TO LOVE AND CHERISH

HOME TO HEATHER CREEK

To Love & Cherish

Leslie Gould

Home to Heather Creek is a trademark of Guideposts.

Copyright © 2023 by Guideposts. All rights reserved.

This book, or parts thereof, may not be reproduced, stored in a retrieval system, or transmitted in any form or by any means, electronic, mechanical, photocopying, recording, or otherwise, without the written permission of the publisher.

The characters and events in this book are fictional, and any resemblance to actual persons or occurrences is coincidental.

Scripture quotations in this volume are taken from the King James Version of the Bible and Holy Bible, New International Version®, NIV® Copyright © 1973, 1978, 1984, 2011 by Biblica, Inc.® Used by permission. All rights reserved worldwide.

Published by Guideposts
100 Reserve Road, Suite E200
Danbury, CT 06810
Guideposts.org

Cover by Lookout Design, Inc.
Interior design by Cindy LaBreacht
Additional design work by Müllerhaus
Typeset by Aptara, Inc.

ISBN 978-1-961125-13-1 (hardcover)
ISBN 978-1-961125-15-5 (epub)

Printed in the United States of America
10 9 8 7 6 5 4 3 2 1

Acknowledgments

I am grateful for the family life I share with my husband Peter and our four children and for the extended family that blesses us. As I was writing *To Love and Cherish*, my brother-in-law and his sweet bride-to-be were in the midst of planning their own wedding. They were always in my thoughts as I wrote this story, and so this book is dedicated to them:

Quy and Sara Gould

—Leslie Gould

Home to Heather Creek

Before the Dawn

Sweet September

Circle of Grace

Homespun Harvest

A Patchwork Christmas

An Abundance of Blessings

Every Sunrise

The Promise of Spring

April's Hope

Seeds of Faith

On the Right Path

Sunflower Serenade

Second Chances

Prayers and Promises

Giving Thanks

Holiday Homecoming

Family Matters

All Things Hidden

To Love and Cherish

… TO LOVE AND CHERISH

Chapter One

Charlotte held the hot cup of tea in her hand and tried to relax against Dana's white sofa. Besides helping Dana plan the wedding, Dana's mother, Bonnie, had been helping her redecorate and had passed down her old living room set. It was in perfect condition—unmarked by children, pets, or dirty work clothes.

"Hey, the wedding is going to be great. Everything will work out." Pete sat beside Dana on the loveseat and held his baseball cap in his hand, a grin spreading across his face.

"Things don't just work out." Bonnie leaned forward. "They have to *be* worked out. *With* planning."

"Mom." Dana was still wearing her church clothes—a navy dress and heels—and her long hair was pulled up in a twist, similar to her mother's, although Bonnie's hair was starting to gray and Dana's was dark and shiny. "Maybe it doesn't need to be done by committee."

"Dana, this is the only way you're going to get what you want. You are wonderful at managing a classroom, dear, but your event-planning skills—" Bonnie stopped abruptly and shrugged.

Charlotte shifted against the back of the couch, feeling as if she'd been caught eavesdropping. Bonnie had invited them—Pete, Charlotte, Emily, and Bob—for Sunday tea at her house in Grand Island, but thankfully Pete had suggested having the gathering in Bedford. Now it was clear that Bonnie's agenda wasn't a social visit for the two families to get to know each other better. No, it seemed that her intention all along had been to host a wedding-planning summit.

"Today's the first of March." Bonnie straightened her wool skirt as she spoke, twisting her full hips just a little. "We have twenty-seven days to pull this off." She reached for a clipboard beside her. "So let's get started."

Bob reached for another cookie. Charlotte gave him a just-one-more look and then reached for another one too. They were shortbread with a hint of hazelnut and chocolate.

"Let's start with the flowers." Bonnie tightened her grip on her clipboard.

Charlotte wasn't sure where her place was as mother of the groom. It had been so easy when Bill, her older son, married Anna. The wedding was at the Lincoln Country Club, and Anna and her mother had handled every detail, never asking for even an opinion from Charlotte. All Charlotte had had to do was buy a dress—approved by Anna, of course—show up for the rehearsal, watch Bob write the check for the dinner afterward, and then enjoy the flawless wedding ceremony and reception the next day.

But this was different. They knew a lot of the same people and for Pete's sake, pun intended, Pete was living in his parents' house. For the time being anyway.

"Charlotte," Bonnie said, "I was asking what you thought of wrist corsages for the mothers."

"Oh," Charlotte replied. "I'm fine with whatever Dana wants."

Bonnie sighed. "Well, that's our problem. Dana doesn't seem to care about the mothers' flowers."

"Then whatever *you* want," Charlotte said.

"Wrist corsages it is, then." Bonnie made a dramatic mark on her list. "What shall we discuss next?" Before anyone could answer she continued. "Ah, yes. The rehearsal dinner." Her eyes landed on Charlotte. "Is everything in order?"

Before Charlotte could speak, Pete cleared his throat and placed his palms flat against the worn fabric of his jeans. "As a matter of fact it is," he said. "We're going to have it at the Riverside Inn. All the reservations have been made, and the menu has been selected."

"Really?" Bonnie said, putting down her pen.

Pete nodded. "Bill and I took care of all of it on Friday. We're having steak and baked potatoes, shrimp kebabs, the whole meal deal." It was quite obvious that Pete was pleased with himself.

Emily wrinkled her nose.

"And a tofu platter for you, little lady." Pete laughed.

"The Riverside Inn? Where is that?" Bonnie shot Dana a look of despair. "Next to that gas station, right? In River Bend?"

"Mother, it will be fine," Dana said. "It's an old place—and nicely redone. Anna, Bill's wife, went to a shower there a few weeks ago. She said it was lovely. And she has good taste."

Charlotte folded her hands in her lap, guessing that comment meant that Bonnie suspected the rest of them *didn't* have good taste.

"All right, then. Although River Bend is a little far to drive." Bonnie peered over the top of the clipboard.

"A half hour's not bad." Pete slouched a little. "And besides, there's nothing available in Bedford that night."

"Well." Bonnie picked up her pen again. "That's what happens when you wait until the last minute."

Charlotte reached for another cookie, determined to change the subject. "Bonnie, you must have a secret ingredient that makes these so delicious."

"It's the hazelnut extract—it's bakery grade." The woman couldn't seem to decide whether to focus on Charlotte or Pete. Fortunately, at that moment Chuck Simons waltzed through the front door.

"Hi, all," he said. "Sorry I'm late." He was a big man, at least six foot three with a balding head, a goatee, and a graceful way about him.

Bonnie's lips pursed together, but Dana leapt to her feet. "Daddy!"

"How's the bride-to-be?" he boomed, giving her a big hug.

"Great. How's the traveling insurance man?"

"A little late." He bent down to Bonnie and kissed her cheek as she swatted her hand at him. "Now don't get started," he said. "I told you I might be running a little behind schedule, pumpkin."

Bonnie frowned.

Charlotte nearly choked on her tea. She couldn't imagine anyone calling Bonnie Simons "pumpkin," not even Chuck.

"Oh, sit down, Chuck." Bonnie sounded gruff, but she was smiling, just a little.

Chuck shook Bob's hand, said hello to Charlotte, and patted Emily on the shoulder. "Pete," he said, sticking out his hand, "I just had lunch with the foreman of that huge corporate farm out on the highway, toward your place. He insisted I stop by when he heard I'd be in the area. He has that tractor you've been pining over."

"Oh, I was just dreamin' out loud," Pete said, glancing at Bob.

"Well, it's a beauty." Chuck smiled and sat down on a dining room chair next to Bonnie.

"Where were we?" Bonnie asked.

Charlotte took a deep breath. Hopefully they were done talking about the rehearsal dinner—and about tractors.

Bonnie tapped her list with the pen. "Oh, yes. The dresses. Emily, are they done?"

Emily's teacup shook a little in her hand as she put it down on the square table next to her. "Almost," she said, her voice faint.

"How close?" Bonnie asked. "I know you haven't done any of the fittings yet. I checked with Michelle."

"Right." Emily scooted to the edge of her chair. She wore a black skirt and a vibrant blue top that made her eyes shine brightly. Her long, blonde hair hung loose on her shoulders. "I'm pretty far along on mine and getting there on the others."

Bonnie smiled. "Okay. So you'll be ready for the fitting with Michelle soon?" Michelle was Dana's cousin who lived in Harding. Her maid of honor was Amber, a friend from college, and she wasn't coming into town until the day before the wedding. She was the difficult one, at least via e-mail.

Emily nodded. "I'll be able to do a fitting for Michelle the night of the shower." She paused. "Or so."

"Do you regret volunteering to make the dresses?" Bonnie held the clipboard to her chest. "It's a big project for a fourteen-year-old."

"Fifteen," Emily said just as the phone rang. "Actually, I'm almost sixteen."

Dana headed to the kitchen, and then her muffled voice grew louder as she walked back into the living room. "Pete, it's Sam."

"Is it the heifer?" Pete jumped up from the loveseat, pulling his hat onto his head.

Dana nodded as she handed him the receiver.

"Sam." Pete spoke loudly. He listened a moment and then said, "I'll be right there." He waved good-bye to everyone as he handed the phone back to Dana. "Sorry to have to leave, but one of my ladies needs me. Sam's getting her in the barn right now."

"Pete, we're nearly done. Can't your nephew handle it?" Bonnie asked, clutching the clipboard with both hands.

"Nope. I gotta go." He turned to Dana and said, "I'll

call," as he hurried out the front door and yanked it shut behind him. They had brought two cars for that very reason. The heifer had been in labor for over a day.

"Well," Bonnie said. "The honeymoon was next on my list. Do you know what your plans are, Dana?"

"Pete says it's a surprise." Dana smiled. "But I'm taking a week off work."

Charlotte avoided Dana's eyes. Was she expecting a true vacation? Pete had told Bob he'd probably only take a few days off because he would be in the middle of seeding.

"Well, well." Bonnie put the clipboard down. "What if one of his ladies needs him on your wedding day? Or during the honeymoon? What then?"

Bob sat up straight, hooking his thumbs into his suspenders. "All the calves will be born by the wedding," he said matter-of-factly. "You see, we bred the cows in—"

"Dana," Charlotte interrupted, "tell me about the reception." She was sure Bonnie did not want to hear a detailed explanation of the breeding of the cows and gestations of the calves.

Dana tucked her feet up on the loveseat. "Well, we're having it at the Goldenrod Bed and Breakfast, as you know—"

Bonnie butted in. "The chef took classes in Lincoln. He's going to make stuffed mushrooms, quiche, crostini—"

"Crostini?" Bob leaned forward. "What in the world?"

Chuck began to smile.

"It's bread—toast—with stuff on it—like tapenade," Emily explained. "I've seen it on the cooking channel at Ashley's."

"Oh, toast," Bob said, leaning back again.

Chuck stood. "We could do that, couldn't we, Bob? Make toast?"

"Chuck." Bonnie gripped her pen tightly. "You're not being helpful."

"Dana, Melody has the cake under control, right?" Charlotte asked.

As Dana talked about the three-layer lemon creation, Charlotte thought about her cake-and-punch reception in the church fellowship hall over forty-six years ago. She concentrated on not sighing. Everything had been so much simpler back then.

AS CHARLOTTE, BOB, AND EMILY stood to leave Dana's home a half hour later, Bonnie took Charlotte's hand. "Thank you so much for coming. I know how busy you are with the farm and your grandkids and your volunteer work and the house."

Charlotte nodded, not quite sure how to take what Bonnie was saying. She turned to Dana and gave her a quick hug and then told Chuck good-bye. As they walked out to Bob's extended-cab pickup, snow began to fall; Emily hurried ahead, clutching her coat around her, before climbing into the backseat of the truck.

"I guess I could have gone to take care of the heifer," Bob said, buckling his seat belt. "Or stayed at the farm in the first place."

Charlotte nodded. He could have gone—and would have—if they had known the agenda for the get-together.

But the thing was, Pete wanted to go back to the farm. Helping birth a calf was way higher on his list of priorities than sitting through an interrogation.

"I thought it went well," Bob said as he backed out of Dana's driveway. "They're nice people."

They were nice people, but still, Charlotte felt uneasy. She turned her head. Emily was chewing on her fingernails.

"Sweetie," Charlotte said. "Stop that."

Emily pulled her hand away. "Oops."

"You okay?"

"Fine."

"How *are* you feeling about the dresses?"

Emily shrugged.

"Exactly how far along are you?" Charlotte twisted a little more toward her granddaughter.

"Grandma, I'll get them done." Emily crossed her arms.

Charlotte faced forward again as Bob turned onto Main Street. The snow was just starting to stick to the road.

"Was this predicted?" Charlotte said.

"I don't think so," Bob replied, accelerating as they left the city limits of Bedford. Large flakes sped toward the windshield. Charlotte leaned back against the seat of the pickup.

Twenty-seven days until the wedding. That wasn't any time at all. She felt unsettled, sure that either she or Pete or Emily—or maybe all three of them—would mess up somehow. Dana, hopefully, would be gracious, but she wasn't so sure about Bonnie. She seemed like a woman on a mission.

Chapter Two

Sam pulled his gloves off his hands and rubbed them together, trying to warm them in the cold of the barn.

"Good job getting the heifer into the barn," Uncle Pete said as he rubbed the beast's belly. "It's really getting cold."

Sam didn't want to let on what a struggle it had been. "It was no problem—even with Christopher trying to help." The heifer hadn't wanted to budge, and he'd had to pull her and prod her to keep her moving while Christopher dangled a handful of alfalfa in front of her nose. Even Toby running in circles and barking hadn't helped.

The ordeal had left Sam chilled to the bone, as Grandma would say. He pulled his gloves back on and then tugged his stocking cap farther down on his head. "How was the get-together with the Simonses?"

Uncle Pete groaned. "Don't ask." He flicked on the lights in the barn.

"That bad?" Sam placed his hands under his armpits.

His uncle nodded, the bill of his baseball cap rising and falling as he turned his attention back to the cow.

Sam took a step toward the window above the heifer's pen. Enough of the last light of day remained for him to see the snowflakes hurtling toward the ground.

"I wonder if the calf is breech," Uncle Pete said, pulling a pair of latex gloves from the box on the barn shelf.

"Is that bad?"

"Yep," Pete said. "We might need the vet."

Sam thought of the night Stormy was born, when the vet had come. It felt like so long ago. They'd only been at Grandma and Grandpa's for a few weeks then, and everything was so new and different. Not like it felt now. "Want me to go call?" Sam said. The vet's number was by the phone.

"Not yet," Uncle Pete said. "I don't want to have to pay for a visit if we don't have—" A burst of water shot out from the backside of the cow.

"Ewww." Sam jumped back.

"Oh, good." His uncle stepped around the heifer and snapped the gloves onto his hands. "This should get things going." The cow stumbled a little and gave out a *moo*.

"There's a hoof." Sam pointed.

"I was right—it's breech."

"How can you tell?" Sam asked.

"It's backward. Usually the front hooves come out first." Uncle Pete's voice was very assured. "Then the head. But that's a back hoof. We're going to have to work fast—otherwise the head will get stuck and the calf will suffocate."

Uncle Pete reached for the hoof and then stepped closer to the cow as Sam turned his head. There were some things he didn't want to see.

The barn door creaked as Sam stepped out of the pen.

"Hey, it's snowing!" Christopher shouted.

"It's always snowing," Sam said. When would it end? He still couldn't get used to the eternal cold.

"Nah, it stopped for a week or so." Christopher grinned. "But it's coming down hard now," he added, hopping toward Sam.

"Shh." Uncle Pete stuck his head out from around the cow. "This is a maternity ward."

Christopher planted his feet at the edge of the pen, yanking his stocking cap off his head. "Is the calf coming?" Christopher's short blond hair stuck up in electric spikes.

"Hopefully." Uncle Pete turned his attention back to the cow. "Hey, do me a favor and go wait for Grandpa. Tell him to get in here as soon as he gets home. Okay?"

"Can't I watch?" Christopher asked.

"Sam—do you want to go wait for Grandpa?"

Sam shook his head. "No. I want to help." At least he thought he wanted to help.

Christopher groaned and headed back to the door.

"Then I need you to stop being squeamish," Uncle Pete said to Sam. "This calf—and cow—are more important than your delicate sensibilities."

"Right," Sam said, not exactly sure what Uncle Pete meant. Every once in a while his uncle surprised him.

"I need you to hold this hoof."

As Sam did what Uncle Pete instructed, he could feel the calf struggling. There was a live creature connected to it, a being that wanted to live. "Shouldn't I go call the vet?" Sam said nervously.

"Too late," Uncle Pete answered as he reached into the cow. "There it is." He pulled out the other hoof.

The cow mooed and stepped forward. "Hold on, girl," Uncle Pete said. "On three. One, two, three."

Sam pulled alongside his uncle, and as the calf slid out to its thighs something stirred in Sam, something he'd never experienced before. He was holding on to a new life; he was witnessing a new being coming into the world.

"Stop." Uncle Pete let go of the hoof and reached inside again. "I don't want the umbilical cord to come out yet." He felt around. The cow mooed. "The calf is pretty little."

Uncle Pete grabbed both legs and pulled, but the calf didn't budge. He let go and wiped his brow with his forearm. "We need to wait for another contraction; then we have to pull hard and fast," he said. Blood covered both of his gloves. Sam concentrated on the little legs of the calf. They had to get it out.

The cow sidestepped again. "Now," Uncle Pete said, grabbing a leg. Sam did the same and together they pulled. Again, the calf didn't budge.

Sam didn't hear the barn door creak, just Grandpa's booming voice. "Heard you're having some trouble." Grandma was right behind him, wearing her church dress and shoes, tottering across the straw-strewn concrete floor.

"It's breech," Uncle Pete said.

"So Doc Trask is on his way?" Grandpa asked.

"Nope," Uncle Pete answered.

The cow mooed.

"Come on, Sam, pull." Uncle Pete put his weight into it this time, pulling hard. Sam tried to do the same.

"Here, son, let me take over." Grandpa was right behind Sam.

Not wanting to relinquish his job, Sam sank his weight against the barn floor. *Come on!* The calf began to slip. Sam pulled harder. The cow bellowed.

"Here it comes," Uncle Pete said, grabbing the calf as it sped, finally, toward the floor.

Sam let go and fell backward against Grandpa's shins, landing on his boots.

"Easy." Grandpa chuckled, catching Sam under his arms.

"Is it breathing?" Grandma asked.

"Not yet." Uncle Pete massaged the calf's chest as the cow turned around and nuzzled the little one.

"It went without air there for a little while," Grandpa said calmly. "Sometimes they don't come back."

Sam kneeled down beside the calf, and Grandma handed him a towel. One of the calf's back legs jerked. Then a front leg. Maybe it was just reflexes. Sam began rubbing the calf's hip as Uncle Pete continued to massage its chest. Its head jerked up.

"He's looking better," Grandpa said.

"He's a little guy; that's for sure." Uncle Pete kept massaging.

"You'd better make sure that afterbirth comes out," Grandpa said. He stood with his coat open and his thumbs in his suspenders, his cap pulled down on his forehead.

"I know." Uncle Pete sounded annoyed.

Grandpa crossed his arms. "Well, do you need me for anything else?"

"Nope. We've got this covered," Uncle Pete answered.

"I can keep helping." Sam continued rubbing the calf, moving the towel over its little black body, watching its face, which was accented by a white rhombus shape between its eyes.

"Thanks." Uncle Pete turned his attention to the cow. "You did good, Sam. I couldn't have done it without you."

Sam warmed inside. It hadn't been as bad as he had thought it would be. And the calf was going to be okay. That's what counted.

The barn door creaked and Sam assumed Christopher was back, but then Emily's voice called out, "Uncle Pete, Miss Simons is on the phone."

Pete groaned. "Tell her I'll call her back."

"She said she really needs to talk with you. She has a question for you—about the wedding."

"I'll talk to her," Grandma said. "I'll tell her you'll call her back as soon as possible."

"Thanks," Uncle Pete muttered.

"GRANDMA SAID TO BRING you a sandwich." Emily stood over Sam several hours later. He hadn't heard her come into the barn again.

"What time is it?"

"Eight-thirty." Emily handed him the plate. "Grandma said you can stay out for another hour, but then you have to come in. She said to tell you that calves have survived for centuries without anyone watching them." Emily smiled and squatted down on the straw. She wore jeans and her Nebraska sweatshirt under Grandma's brown coat.

Sam bit into the ham sandwich, straight into a dill pickle. He chewed quickly and swallowed, and then took another bite. He hadn't realized how hungry he was.

"The snow is really piling up," Emily said, rubbing the calf's head.

Sam nodded. He'd looked out the barn door an hour ago.

"What are you going to name the little guy?" Emily sat down cross-legged.

Sam shrugged. He wasn't sure if he wanted to name it.

"Uncle Pete's been calling it Snowflake—'cause of the mark on its head," Emily said.

"Snowflake," Sam echoed, his mouth full. "That works."

"Has he nursed yet?" Emily took the plate from Sam and stood.

"Nope. He's still pretty weak."

"Uncle Pete will be back when he's done talking to Miss Simons. He said the calf needs to drink its mom's milk to get something or other or the little guy won't make it." Emily patted the cow's back.

Sam nodded. Uncle Pete had told him that too, but Sam wasn't going to do anything to make that happen. He could sit with the calf, but the other stuff was up to Uncle Pete.

"Arielle was at youth group," Emily said.

"You went?" Sam hadn't been for a few weeks.

"Yep. With Ashley."

"How were the roads?"

"Fine."

"So, no chance of school being canceled tomorrow?"

Emily rolled her eyes. "Come on, Sam. This is Nebraska, remember? They'll just put chains on the buses."

She was right. School rarely got canceled around here. And it had already happened once this winter.

"How's Arielle?" Sam asked.

"Fine. Interested in the calf."

"Really?" Sam hoped he didn't sound too enthusiastic. He'd been missing her lately. Sure, she'd been acting really weird by the time they broke up, but he missed talking with her. She'd been his best friend for all that time.

Emily pulled her hat down over her ears. "I told her all about the birth. How you practically delivered it by yourself. How you saved its—"

"Emily."

She wrinkled her nose. "I just told her you were home helping Uncle Pete, that's all."

"Oh." He would have been okay with her telling Arielle about the calf.

Emily left, and fifteen minutes later Uncle Pete reappeared, slamming the barn door shut and stomping the snow from his boots.

"How's Snowflake doing?"

"Still sleeping." Sam had been watching the calf's chest rise and fall.

"We'd better get him up." Uncle Pete slid his arms underneath the calf. "Dinner's right over here, fella," he said.

Snowflake opened one eye and then the other as Uncle Pete put him on his feet and then scooted him over to his mom, nudging her udder. Uncle Pete let go, and Snowflake started to fall. Sam grabbed him.

"No, let him be."

Sam obeyed, putting his arms behind his back.

Snowflake fell to the floor, closing his eyes again. The cow started to nuzzle him, licking his nose and face.

"Maybe he needs a bottle," Sam said.

"He needs to nurse." Uncle Pete tried again, but Snowflake wouldn't or couldn't stand on his feet. Nor could he seem to stay awake.

After twenty minutes of trying, Uncle Pete headed back to the house to mix up a bottle of calf formula that was left over from last year. Grandma came back with him, a big plastic bottle in her hand, offering to take over the feeding so Sam could get ready for bed.

Grandma dribbled milk onto Snowflake's nose and mouth, and he started sucking on the nipple.

"Can I do it, please?" Sam asked.

Grandma relented after he assured her that he didn't have any homework.

"We'll get him nursing in the morning," Uncle Pete said. "After he's had a chance to get his strength back."

"You don't think he was too oxygen-deprived?" Grandma asked as she followed Uncle Pete to the door.

"Nah. He's just small. And weak. His sucking reflexes are there. He'll be okay, even if he lost a few brain cells."

Sam held the bottle as Snowflake drank down the formula with his eyes closed. The cow turned toward her calf. Sam reached over and rubbed her head. She nuzzled his hand with her nose. It was warm and dry.

He'd get up early with Uncle Pete and help with Snowflake. He sighed, surprised at what a good day it had been. Grandma always said that true satisfaction came from helping others. She was right.

Chapter Three

Charlotte stirred under the down comforter and turned her head toward the clock. 3:15 AM. She was half awake, thinking about Bonnie Simons's expectations. But she felt uneasy about something else too, more than just the wedding. Charlotte yawned, swinging her legs over the side of the bed. She might as well get up and go to the bathroom, and then maybe she could fall back into a deep sleep.

She shivered as she pulled her robe over her flannel nightgown and then stepped into her slippers. The uneasy feeling increased as she headed down the hall. She would check on the kids first. Maybe one of them was ill. Denise used to tease Charlotte that she was like Miss Clavel in the *Madeline* books, able to sense a sick child in the night.

Tiptoeing up the stairs, Charlotte trailed her fingers along the handrail. Light bouncing off the snow-covered landscape filled the window over the landing. She stopped, taking in the winter wonderland. It wasn't unheard-of to get a complete blanketing of snow in March, but it was unusual. And the temperature had dropped—just twenty-two degrees when she went to bed. She glanced out the window when she reached the landing. Funny, it looked as if a light was on in the barn.

She headed on up the stairs and down the hall, gently pressing open Christopher's door. He was sound asleep in his bed, tucked under his brown quilt, his head turned toward the wall. She didn't venture in any farther, not wanting to wake him up.

Next, she eased Emily's door open. Her granddaughter slept with her arms over her head, flung across the top of her pillow. She stirred a little and Charlotte pulled the door shut. She must have been imagining things, thinking she'd seen a light on in the barn. She opened Sam's door and peered into the dark room, waiting a second for her eyes to adjust. The blankets were pulled back. The bed was empty.

For a second she thought about rousing Pete out of the spare bedroom and asking him to go look for Sam, but maybe he was just down in the kitchen or perhaps he was on the computer. He wouldn't go too far on a night like this.

Charlotte hurried down the stairs and through the family room. No Sam. He wasn't in the kitchen either. She stopped at the kitchen window. The light was definitely on in the barn. Maybe he'd gone out there to check on the calf.

Sam had hardly shown any interest in farm life all this time, and suddenly he was bonding with that little calf. Hopefully Snowflake would make it. Charlotte shivered again and hurried to the back porch, pulled her coat on over her bathrobe, and then kicked off her slippers and wiggled her feet into her boots. She remembered being a young girl on her grandparents' farm and coming across her first dead calf. She had cried and cried. She had been younger than Sam was now, of course; but still, any time you cared for a creature it was really hard to have it die.

Flinging open the back door, she stepped out into the night. Sure enough, footprints larger than hers dotted the backyard. She stepped into each one, stretching her stride, holding up her robe as she trudged along. She tilted her head heavenward. The sky was clear now, the stars bright. She crossed the driveway and hurried on to the barn, pushing her weight against the door as she unlatched it.

"Sam?" she called out.

"Am I in trouble?" He stepped into the middle of the barn, his down jacket unbuttoned over a T-shirt and sweatpants, his brown curls flattened against his head.

Charlotte smiled. "How is Snowflake?"

"Sleeping." Sam ducked back into the pen, and Charlotte followed him, glancing at the calf, taking in the rise and fall of his little chest. She smiled until she registered that the cow was on her side. Charlotte stepped toward her.

The cow didn't move. Charlotte felt her nose. It was burning hot and dry. Charlotte squatted against the beast, feeling the cow's stomach. "Sam," she said calmly, "go wake Pete. Tell him the cow is down."

"Down?" Sam stood beside her. "What do you mean?"

"Go get Pete, honey."

"Is she dead?" Sam kneeled beside the cow.

"Not yet." Charlotte turned toward her grandson. "Go get Pete, okay?"

Forty-five minutes later Doc Trask emptied a syringe of antibiotics into the cow. "We'll know in a few hours," he said. "Hopefully this will bring her around."

Sam looked as if he was going to cry.

"Keep feeding the calf from the bottle or graft him onto another cow," the vet said. "Even if this cow makes it, her milk is apt to be low."

"I'll go fix a bottle," Charlotte said. There was no way they were going to graft a runt of a calf like Snowflake to another cow on a night like this.

"Let me do it, Grandma."

"No, you go back to bed." Charlotte put her arm around Sam. "Get some sleep, and you can give him his morning bottle." Maybe that thought would give Sam the incentive he would need to get up in a few short hours.

THE SUN WAS ON ITS WAY over the horizon when Charlotte pushed up the sleeves of her sweater and began lining the frying pan with strips of bacon.

Sam stumbled into the kitchen. "How's the calf?" he asked.

"Okay." Charlotte nodded toward the bottle on the counter. "Waiting for you, I'm sure."

"I'm on my way," Sam said, grabbing the bottle and heading toward the door.

"Wait." Charlotte stepped away from the stove. "The cow didn't make it, sweetie."

Sam stopped at the door. "Where is she?"

"Behind the barn. Your uncle will bury her later this morning." The ground had thawed before this latest snow; hopefully it hadn't frozen again.

Sam stepped back into the kitchen and sat down at the table. Charlotte put her hand on his shoulder as Pete burst through the back door, stomping his feet and clapping his gloved hands together. "Nothing like bitter cold to make up for a lack of sleep," he boomed, hanging his coat. He headed into the kitchen as Charlotte turned her attention back to the bacon.

"I hate it when an animal dies." Pete poured himself a cup of coffee.

"It's part of being a farmer," Charlotte answered.

"I don't get it," Sam said.

"Get what?" Pete sat down.

Sam pushed the bottle to the middle of the table. "Why anyone would want to be a farmer."

Charlotte put the last piece of bacon down. "This doesn't happen very often—but both birth and death are part of life."

Sam stared straight ahead.

Charlotte winced. She didn't need to tell that to a boy who had lost his mother when he was sixteen.

"Hey." Pete nudged Sam. "Snowflake still needs his bottle."

"And you'd better hurry," Charlotte said. "You'll need to ride the bus. I don't want you driving this morning; there's no guarantee that the plows have gone through."

Sam stood, bumping his chair back, and then stumbled to the door.

"Your coat—" Charlotte called out.

"Let him go," Pete said. "He'll be all right."

AFTER THE CHILDREN LEFT to catch the bus, it started to snow again. Pete and Bob sat at the table drinking another round of coffee while Charlotte washed the calf's bottles, pushing the brush in and out of the lemony dishwater as it grew more bubbles.

"What do you have planned for today?" Bob asked Pete.

"Besides firing up the backhoe and burying a cow?"

Bob nodded.

"I was thinking about going into Harding to look at tractors. Ours can't last much longer."

"Ours is fine." Bob pushed his chair back. "Besides, we can't afford a new tractor."

"I know. But it doesn't hurt to look."

"No." Bob paused. "Sometimes it does hurt to look."

Pete scowled and stood, leaving his coffee cup on the table.

The kettle whistled, and Charlotte turned off the burner. "I'll give Snowflake his next bottle," she said, but Pete was already through the door.

Bob took a long drink of coffee and then put his cup down. "We can't afford any new equipment at all right now."

"He knows that. Maybe he just needs a break." Charlotte poured the boiling water over the bottles to sterilize them.

Bob grunted. "A break? That's the problem, don't you think? All this wedding planning is taking him away from his farming. He was on the phone with Dana for an hour last night when he should have been out in the barn making sure the cow was all right."

"Sam was out there."

"What does Sam know about cows?"

Charlotte sat down across the table from her husband. "But you can't blame the cow's dying on Pete."

Bob shrugged.

"Honey, you've had cows die."

"Not many."

"Still."

"Still? It was a healthy heifer. Do you know how much money we just lost?"

Charlotte stood and lifted the bottles out of the hot water, positioning them on the rack. Bob's response was most likely about more than just the cow. She stole a look at him.

He clasped his hands together around his coffee cup. He looked a little lost. "I'm not ready to be sent out to pasture —yet," he said, as though he were reading her thoughts. Then he frowned. "I probably should have been more involved yesterday."

"It wouldn't have mattered," Charlotte said.

Bob didn't answer, so she changed the subject. "It's been nice to see Sam take an interest in the calf."

Bob nodded, his chin bobbing against his thick neck.

Sam's interest made her think of Denise, how eager she had been to help take care of the calves and the foals. How much she had liked hand-feeding them. She expected it from Emily but was surprised to see Sam rise to the occasion.

She pulled the sink plug, turning her thoughts toward lunch. She could make soup, but she would need chicken stock, and she'd used the last of the frozen stock in the freezer the day before. What she really needed to do was the grocery shopping, even more so if a second storm was on the way, as predicted. Charlotte turned toward Bob. "Want to go into town with me?"

He shook his head.

"I could use help with the groceries."

"I guess I could check with Brad about when the seed is coming in," Bob said.

Charlotte grabbed the hand towel. "We could eat lunch at Mel's Place."

Bob stretched his arms. "That's not necessary."

"Of course it's not," Charlotte said, drying her hands. "But it would be nice."

A puzzled look spread over Bob's face. "It would be nice to eat here too."

Charlotte hung up the towel as she spoke. "Could you humor me? I'm low on groceries and am having a hard time thinking of something to fix for lunch. And we won't go broke if we treat ourselves now and then."

A SHORT WHILE LATER Bob swung open the door to Mel's Place for Charlotte, and they stepped in from the cold, kicking the snow off their boots. The café was nearly full and loud with conversation. It seemed half the town had had the same idea as Charlotte.

She breathed in the scent of coffee as she unbuttoned her wool coat. For a second she thought she heard her name. She looked around the room. Mel was waiting on a customer at the counter. Charlotte heard her name again but didn't recognize the voice.

"Over here!" It was Bonnie Simons, waving her arm from the far corner of the café. She was sitting with Chuck's mother, Maxine, who was called Grandma Maxie by practically everyone in town.

Making her way across the room, around the tables decorated with vases of silk tulips, Charlotte stopped in her tracks, surprised to see Hannah and Frank.

"A little hard to plant in this, isn't it?" Frank said to Bob.

"Well, I probably could handle it," Bob joked, "but Pete can't seem to figure it out."

Hannah reached out her hand for Charlotte's. "Why don't you sit with us?"

Charlotte thought nothing would be lovelier than having lunch with her best friend.

"Charlotte!" It was Bonnie again.

"Oh," Hannah said. "You're meeting Bonnie and Grandma Maxie." Charlotte didn't clarify the situation. "Go on," Hannah said. "We can talk later."

Charlotte leaned down and gave her friend a hug and continued weaving her way around the tables with Bob in tow. "Should we sit with Bonnie?" she whispered.

"Probably," he answered.

"Is Pete with you?" Bonnie wore a blazer and slacks, and her wedding-planning clipboard was on the table in front of her.

Charlotte shook her head, and then both she and Bob greeted Grandma Maxie.

"What's Pete up to?" Bonnie asked as Charlotte wiggled down into her chair.

"He's off to Harding," Bob said, pushing in Charlotte's chair.

Bonnie beamed. "Oh, good. Dana told him he needed to get fitted for his tuxedo."

"Tuxedo?" Bob extended his hands flat on the table. "He was talking about tractors when he left."

Charlotte put her hand on Bob's forearm. "Well, he was probably going to do that too, dear."

"We had a cow die last night." Bob said.

"Oh, that's too bad," Grandma Maxie responded, genuine concern in her sweet voice.

Bonnie looked from Bob to Charlotte. "That happens on a farm, right?"

"From time to time," Bob said. "But this is the heifer who just calved yesterday, and now we have a calf that's at risk too."

"Still," Bonnie continued. "It's all part of farm life, right?"

Charlotte realized she had a smile frozen on her face. She blinked. She had practically told Sam the same thing just a few hours ago, but hearing Bonnie Simons say it made her uneasy.

"But a wedding happens only once—right?" Bonnie folded her hands together and placed them on top of the clipboard.

Grandma Maxie looked a little bewildered and took a breath as if she might say something, but instead she patted the salt-and-pepper bun at the nape of her neck.

"Well." Charlotte paused. "I think we can do both—keep the farm going and plan a wedding." Bonnie didn't seem to realize that the farm had to come first. Being responsible for livestock had a different level of involvement than other jobs.

"The farm can't be neglected," Bob said. "Especially not this time of year. For example, Pete was on the phone—"

Charlotte nudged him under the table with her boot.

"—with Dana when that cow started to fail—"

This time Charlotte poked him.

"—when he should have been out in the—"

"Coffee for all?" Mel stood beside their table, her red apron brushed with flour, her dishwater-blonde hair pulled back in a ponytail.

"Please!" Charlotte knew she'd answered with too much enthusiasm. As Mel made her way around the table, Charlotte turned to Bonnie. "Tell us what you and Dana decided about the flowers. Every last detail. I'm dying to know."

"Well, actually we haven't decided that, but I have come to another decision. I'm going to move in with Dana until the wedding."

Charlotte felt her eyes grow wide as Bob choked a little on his coffee. Grandma Maxie nodded her head gently as if trying to convince Charlotte that Bonnie was serious.

"I stayed last night, as planned. And then just this morning I told Dana I might as well stay the rest of the month. I'm going back to Grand Island this afternoon to get my things."

"Well, well," Charlotte managed to say.

"She needs my help," Bonnie said. "There's no doubt about it." Her eyes welled up a little. "And she's my only child. This will be my last chance to be with her."

As Charlotte forced a smile she wondered how Pete would respond to Bonnie's plan.

Chapter Four

Emily fled her classroom as the bell rang, determined to get out to the bus as soon as possible. If anyone asked her what the hurry was, she'd say she needed to get a good seat so she didn't get stuck in the back with the middle school boys; but the truth was she didn't want to run into Miss Simons in the hall. It wasn't that her uncle's fiancée had turned into Bridezilla—not exactly. Emily just didn't want her to ask about the dresses.

As her boots clicked on the linoleum of the hall, she zipped up her sweatshirt and slipped her notebook into her book bag.

"Hey, Em." It was Sam. "Don't miss the bus." He was headed toward the front door already.

"I'll be right there." She hurried to her locker, grabbed her down coat, and quickly shoved her arms through the sleeves. Then she turned her attention to her locker, searching for her history book and dislodging a fashion magazine on the top shelf. It tumbled down, hitting her head.

"Ouch." She picked it up and then rubbed her scalp, dropping the magazine onto the bottom of her locker. Why had she ever volunteered to make the dresses? It was crazy of her, really. Why had Grandma and Dana agreed to it? They should have known better than to let a fifteen-year-old take on such an important task.

Ashley came up beside her as Emily dug around on the top shelf for her book.

"Want to come over? I don't work today." Ashley wore a knit orange-and-purple beanie hat. Her red curls spilled over her shoulders.

Emily shook her head. "Nah. I need to work on the bridesmaids' dresses."

"How are they coming along?"

"Fine." Emily slammed her locker and Ashley put her hand on Emily's shoulder.

Emily couldn't fool Ashley. "Not," Emily said. "I don't know why I said I'd do it."

"But you're really good. You're probably just having a confidence crisis."

Emily wrinkled her nose.

Ashley smiled. "Can I help? Not with the sewing. You're so much better than I am—but I could cut or press or something."

Emily shook her head. "I just need to buckle down and get going on them."

"How much do you have done?"

"Some."

"Emily?"

She shrugged.

"Exactly how much more do you have to do?" Ashley asked, opening her locker.

Emily groaned. "I've barely started."

"You've barely started what?" It was Miss Simons, standing in the middle of the hall with her arms crossed. Her hair was pulled up on her head and looked like she hadn't washed it for a day or two. She wore the same outfit she'd had on yesterday afternoon.

Emily's gaze of desperation landed on Ashley.

"Art project," Ashley said. "And Emily has been so busy with—with the wedding stuff—that she's barely started."

Miss Simons put her arm around Emily. "Whew. For a minute I thought you were talking about the bridesmaids' dresses."

As Emily shook her head, a sick feeling rose in the back of her throat.

Miss Simons gave her a squeeze. "Don't let me down, sweetie. I've got too much to stress about as it is."

Emily nodded and pulled away, and Miss Simons continued down the hall. Was she muttering to herself?

"I'll walk you to the parking lot," Ashley said. As they pushed through the double doors of the school into the cold, Ashley whispered, "I didn't mean to lie to Miss Simons. It just came out."

"We do have an art project that's due." Emily wasn't even going to think about that or her other homework right now. Why had Pete and Miss Simons decided to get married in March? What was wrong with June?

"Hurry up!" Sam stood on the steps of the bus.

"Thanks, Ashley," Emily said, giving her friend a hug. "I'll see you tomorrow."

Emily settled onto the front seat of the full bus, close to

the heater. In a couple of minutes the snow on her boots melted into a puddle of water that ran along the grooves of the floor. The noise of the younger kids escalated as the bus turned onto the highway, and she shifted around in her seat. Two eighth-grade boys were tossing a wad of paper back and forth. At least Christopher wasn't involved. He was sitting behind her with Sam.

"Want to build a snowman when we get home?" Christopher asked Sam.

Emily sighed. Wasn't he sick of the snow? They'd only had a couple of weeks without it.

"I'm going to feed Snowflake," Sam said.

"Can I help?"

"Sure," Sam answered.

Emily turned back around. Sam and Christopher got to have all the fun. All she had to look forward to when she got home were those royal blue dresses.

"DO YOU WANT TO WORK down here?" Grandma sat at the dining room table, peeling potatoes. "We can turn the family room into a sewing center."

"Nah," Emily said. "I can do it in my room." She headed toward the stairs, both hands gripping the handle of the case, the sewing machine bumping around inside of it. She took the stairs lopsided, the case slamming against her shin as she made her way up one step at a time. She didn't want to work downstairs because then Grandma would see how much more she still had to do. She'd only cut out her own dress and pressed the fabric for the other dresses. She would get started sewing hers before dinner and cut out the other two dresses after dinner.

She turned the doorknob to her bedroom and kicked the door open as the late afternoon light cast a pall over her room. She swung the sewing machine onto her desk and opened her curtain. Dark clouds hung heavily in the sky, and shadows crept across the snow-covered landscape. It was going to storm again by nightfall. If only school would get canceled tomorrow—then she would have time to sew. Then she could make some progress.

After setting up the machine she concentrated on her dress. She had pretty much completed the design of the dresses, but then the maid of honor, Amber, wanted sleeves added. Emily had found a pattern with cap sleeves and used it to adapt what she had already designed. She pulled out the directions of the pattern with the sleeves. She'd pinned them into place but they didn't look right; the fabric bunched up funny. She read the directions for the sleeves again but all it said was to baste the fabrics together, which she'd already done. She placed the fabric under the foot of her machine and began to sew.

Two hours later she was ripping the right sleeve out—again—when Christopher banged on her bedroom door. "Time for dinner!" he yelled.

"Just a minute," Emily shouted back.

"No, now!" The door crashed open. Christopher held his stocking cap in his hands. His face was red, his cheeks chapped.

Emily put down the fabric and seam ripper. She'd hardly gotten anything done. In fact, things had gone from bad to worse. First, she hadn't had the machine's tension set right. So the sleeve bunched up and she had to rip it out. Then the sleeve bunched up even more when she sewed it the second time. Then she'd torn a hole in the fabric as she was ripping out the seam.

She followed Christopher down the stairs. Hopefully things would go better after dinner.

LATER THAT EVENING, Emily sat in the middle of her room and stretched her aching back. Four hours of sewing and she'd made hardly any progress. The cut pieces of fabric for Michelle's dress surrounded her as she held her own dress in her hands.

She'd resewn the sleeves, but they still didn't look right. She stood and dropped the dress on her bed and shuffled over to her window. It was snowing fast and furiously. She wondered if Sam or Uncle Pete had given Snowflake his nighttime bottle. She sighed and then tiptoed around the pieces of fabric and opened her door, closing it securely so that the cat couldn't come in. The last thing she needed was for Lightning to come in and have a field day with the fabric.

She started down the stairs. Maybe she could feed the calf.

Grandma, wearing her bathrobe, and Uncle Pete were sitting at the dining room table. Emily glanced at the kitchen clock. 9:05 PM. "Is Sam feeding Snowflake?" Emily asked.

Uncle Pete nodded.

"I think I'll go out," Emily said.

"How's the sewing going?" Grandma asked, standing.

"Fine." Emily grabbed her down jacket.

"Do you want Rosemary to help you? I'm sure she would."

Emily shook her head. "I think I can handle it." She still felt bad about not buying the fabric at Aunt Rosemary's shop. Aunt Rosemary didn't carry what Miss Simons wanted and Emily had been afraid it would take too long to order it from Fabrics and Fun.

"Could you show me what you've gotten done?" Grandma shot a glance at Uncle Pete as she spoke.

Emily pulled her hat and gloves out of her jacket pocket. "I will—tomorrow." She opened the back door. "I'll be right back," she called over her shoulder, yanking the door shut. Toby stuck her head out of her doghouse but stayed put.

The wind howled and the snow swirled around Emily, stinging her face as she hurried down the path lined by two banks of snow. There had to be almost a foot on the ground by now. She struggled with the barn door, pushing her weight against it, suddenly desperate to get in. She hadn't been out to see Stormy for days. She hadn't even asked Uncle Pete how the horses were doing. The door swung open and she fell against it, staggering into the barn.

"Hey, shut it quick. It's freezing out there." Sam's voice was sharp and commanding.

Emily obeyed and then walked toward him. "How's it going?" she asked.

"He seems okay. Uncle Pete's not so sure—but he's hungry and he drinks all of his milk."

Emily squatted down beside Sam. A week ago Sam would have been cynical. She could imagine him saying the calf was going to die anyway—either now or in two years at the slaughterhouse.

As the calf jerked on the bottle, Sam lifted it higher, forcing the milk down. Emily reached out and rubbed the calf's head, but he turned away, loosening his grip on the bottle.

"Em." Sam was annoyed. "Back off, would you? You're distracting him."

Emily scooted back again. "It's awfully cold in here."

"Yep." Sam repositioned the bottle and Snowflake began sucking again. "Uncle Pete said I can't bring him into the house though."

"Sam."

"What?"

Emily laughed. "You're kidding."

"No." It was obvious he wasn't.

Not even Emily had asked to bring any of the livestock into the house. "Who's giving him his middle-of-the-night bottle?"

"Me." Sam hesitated. "If Grandma will let me. Uncle Pete said I could, but I have to pass it by her."

Emily felt a pang of jealousy. She stood and walked down to the other end of the barn, kicking at strands of straw, breathing in the musty smell of dust mixed with oats and hay. A swallow flew out of its nest high in the rafters and then settled down again. Stormy nickered when she saw Emily, and Emily began stroking the mare's forehead.

Grandma couldn't seem to stop asking if she needed help. Emily didn't want to ask Aunt Rosemary because then everyone would know how little she had done, but maybe someone else could help her. Maybe Ashley could come over and cut out the third dress while Emily sewed. That might be just the help she needed. She headed back through the barn. She would ask Grandma if Ashley could come tomorrow, after school.

In three more weeks she wouldn't have to worry about the dresses. In three more weeks Miss Simons would be her aunt. It was hard to fathom either thought.

Chapter Five

Charlotte watched the children walk up the drive as she listened to Bill over the phone. "I'm telling you, Mom, he's a smart little baby. And strong. He's rolling everywhere now and laughing, especially at Jennifer. And Madison carries him all over the house."

Bill was going on like little Will was the first baby—well, first baby boy—ever born.

"Of course, Anna gets a little nervous about the girls carrying him, but I think they're doing okay." Bill paused for a moment.

"That's great that you helped Pete book the place for the rehearsal dinner," Charlotte said.

"Well, you know Pete. Anna and I were afraid he'd never get it done without some help. Anna's worried that he's going to drive Dana crazy." Bill chuckled.

Charlotte winced and turned toward the window, focusing on the kids. Sam lobbed a snowball at Christopher. Emily was straggling behind. Charlotte squinted. Ashley was with her.

"Mom?"

Oops. She'd stopped listening to Bill. "Could you say that last bit again?" He was on his cell phone way out in Monroe County.

"I was just saying that business has been a little slow."

"That's too bad—but probably to be expected, right?" Surely the law business wasn't recession-proof either. "Hey, the kids just got home. I'll talk to you soon, okay?"

They said their good-byes and Charlotte opened the door. The day had turned bright and the snow sparkled, nearly blinding her.

"Do you have Snowflake's bottle ready?" Sam asked, hurrying through the door first.

"Not yet," Charlotte said. The calf had seemed a little stronger at noon. Even Pete thought so.

The phone rang again just as Christopher, Emily, and Ashley hustled through the door. It was Dana, asking for Pete.

"He's out in the shop, working on the tractor," Charlotte said. Bob was out there too. She hadn't seen any wrenches flying out the door so she assumed Pete hadn't brought up buying a new tractor again.

Emily and Ashley slowly slipped off their boots and took off their coats. Charlotte moved toward the family room.

"Do you know if he got fitted for his tux yet?" Dana asked.

Charlotte didn't think he had.

"Can he go today?"

Charlotte said she wasn't sure.

"What about tomorrow?" Dana sounded tired. "Sam and Christopher too. Maybe Emily could go with them to make sure they all get fitted. So we know for sure they did."

"Oh, that probably won't be necessary."

"I think maybe it is," Dana said.

"I'll have Pete call," she answered. "Right away." She didn't want to get in the middle of this. As she hung up the phone, she realized Emily was watching her.

"Everything okay?" Emily asked. She wore jeans, and her hair was in braids.

"Fine. How about the dresses? Everything okay there?" Charlotte sat down at the table.

"Please don't nag." Emily planted her hands on her hips. "You've asked me about the dresses three times in the last twenty-four hours."

Charlotte was surprised it had been only three. If Emily only knew how many times she had bitten her tongue. She sighed. It would be a little hard for Emily to work on the dresses tomorrow and go to Harding with the boys. Maybe Charlotte should go. Then she'd know for sure that Pete was taking care of everything. She grimaced. She had given up trying to control Pete years ago, and now here she was, tempted to go back to that.

Charlotte smiled at her granddaughter. "I know you'll get the dresses done, sweetie."

Emily frowned. "I think with Ashley here I'll get a lot done. She's going to..." Emily paused and then added, "help."

Charlotte tilted her head. "Help?"

Ashley stood in the dining room archway. "Cut out a dress."

"Emily." Charlotte turned toward her granddaughter. "I thought you said all the dresses were cut out."

Emily shook her head. "No, I didn't say that. Not exactly."

She took a step toward the hall. "Come on, Ashley. Let's get to work." Emily's words were followed by the thunder of footsteps going up the stairs.

Charlotte measured the calf formula into a bottle, trying to remember if Emily had actually said all the dresses were cut out or just implied it. She peered through the kitchen window again. The boys were back outside, pelting each other with snowballs. Christopher spun around, taking a hit in the middle of his back. Sam hurled another one at his little brother and began laughing. It was hard for her to tell when they were still having fun and when it was getting out of hand.

She shook the bottle before she put on her coat, hat, and gloves.

A couple of minutes later she dodged snowballs as she trod along the path of snow through the backyard. "Hey, Sam. Stop a minute," she yelled, grasping the bottle in her gloved hand. She'd wrapped it in a dishtowel, hoping to keep it warm.

"Can I feed Snowflake?" Christopher asked, dropping his snowball.

"It's my turn." Sam lobbed one last sphere of snow at his brother.

"It's Christopher's turn," Charlotte said, walking along the path that Pete had shoveled. Sam scowled, and then both boys fell into step with her, tramping through the snow.

"You boys need to go to Harding tomorrow with Pete to get fitted for your tuxes."

"For *what*?" Christopher asked.

Sam made a face. "It's a stupid monkey suit."

"Sam." Charlotte shook her head. That was all she needed. "It's a nice suit. It's a privilege to wear one."

Christopher groaned. "I'm just showing people where to sit, right? Why do I have to wear a suit?"

"So you'll look nice when you trip some old lady." Sam chuckled.

Christopher frowned and then ran ahead and pushed open the barn door. Charlotte increased her stride and Sam started to jog, leaving her behind.

"Eeew!" Christopher's voice sounded like it was coming from a cave.

Charlotte secured the barn door behind her.

Sam stood beside Snowflake's pen, his nose plugged. In a nasal tone he said, "Somebody's sick."

"Go get Pete. He's in the tractor shed," Charlotte said to Christopher, looking around the straw-covered floor of the calf's pen. From the looks of things, the formula was going right through Snowflake. She nudged Sam's elbow. "You can help me clean the little guy up."

"Grandma," Sam wailed, the nasal tone even more pronounced.

"Come on, let's get him over to the hose." Charlotte took off her leather gloves and replaced them with rubber ones from the supply shelf. "Come on. Now." Charlotte snapped the latex into place.

"Do I have to?"

"I can't do it by myself."

Sam pulled gloves onto his hands and lifted the calf from the hay, turning his head to the side. As he put

Snowflake on his feet, the animal's knobby knees shook a little, but he followed Sam down to the end of the barn.

"The soap is on that back shelf," Charlotte said. "I'm going to get rid of this hay and then I'll come help." She gathered the soiled straw with the pitchfork and then stepped out of the pen. Snowflake was nuzzling Sam's legs as Sam tried to rinse off the calf's backside with warm water.

Charlotte emptied her load of straw into the wheelbarrow and was spreading fresh hay in the calf's pen when Christopher led Bob and Pete into the barn.

"Go get a couple of old towels," Charlotte said to Christopher. "They're on the shelf in the laundry room. And a bucket of warm water."

Pete and Bob gathered around the calf. "Do we still have some of that baby stuff—that clear liquid?" Pete asked.

"The electrolyte drink?" Charlotte asked, taking a break and leaning against a splintery post in the middle of the barn. They'd given it to a calf a couple of years ago, and it had helped.

"Yep. That's the stuff."

Charlotte shook her head. "No."

"I'm thinking this little guy needs some of that." Pete reached down and took the calf's black head in his hands. "Or we could call the vet."

"Not yet," Bob said. "Let's see how your idea works."

"Want to ride along with me, squirt?" Pete said to Christopher.

"Get a loaf of bread too," Charlotte said. "Please." She'd meant to start a couple of loaves but hadn't gotten around to it.

Christopher ran ahead of Pete, swinging open the barn

door. As Charlotte went back to spreading fresh straw, she realized she hadn't told Pete that Dana had called. She would tell him as soon as he got back, before dinner. That would give him plenty of time to return her call.

THE HEARTY AROMA of the pot roast followed Charlotte up the steps to the second floor. She was afraid dinner was going to be overcooked if she didn't get everyone rounded up soon. She'd sent Christopher out to the barn after Sam and then to the shop for Pete and Bob.

She knocked softly on Emily's door. When there was no answer, she knocked harder.

"Who is it?" Emily's voice was sharp.

Charlotte started to turn the doorknob.

"What do you want?" Now Emily's voice was shrill.

"It's time to eat," Charlotte said through the inch of open doorway.

"We'll be right down." Emily answered again, this time even louder.

Charlotte eased the door open a little more. She wasn't sure the light was good enough for the girls to sew, but Emily sat at her desk, guiding a piece of fabric along, the motor of the sewing machine making a steady whir. Charlotte's eyes fell on Ashley, who sat in the middle of the floor with pattern pieces pinned to the fabric spread in front of her, a pair of scissors in her hand. Charlotte pushed the door all the way open.

Ashley bit her lower lip.

"What's wrong?" Charlotte asked.

"I messed up," Ashley said.

"What?" Emily turned away from the machine and stumbled to her feet.

Ashley held up two sleeves. "I think I cut the right sleeve backward."

"Ashley!" Emily spun around.

"No reason to get alarmed," Charlotte said, stepping over the panel of a dress spread out in front of the door. "This sort of thing happens all the time to seamstresses." The pieces of a third dress were spread across Emily's bed.

Emily crossed her arms.

"Is there more fabric?" Charlotte asked.

Ashley rummaged around behind her and then held up a piece of the material. "There's this." It hardly looked big enough for the pattern piece, let alone to cut it to account for the nap of the fabric.

"That's not going to work." Emily sank back down onto her chair. "I can't believe this. Miss Simons is going to freak," she wailed.

"Emily, it's okay," Charlotte said. "We can deal with this." She inhaled, trying to stay calm herself. She reached for the fabric and pattern piece, taking them from Ashley. As soon as she held the pieces in her hand it was obvious that the fabric piece wasn't large enough, but she smiled anyway. "Let's go eat and then deal with this after dinner," Charlotte said. Emily had that wild look in her eyes.

"I'm sorry," Ashley said again, standing.

"No worries," Charlotte said. "Come along, girls." She patted Ashley's back as the girl headed through the door, and then put her hand firmly on Emily's forearm. "Sweetie," she whispered, ushering her out the door, "being kind to Ashley is far more important than working on the dresses."

Emily wrinkled her nose, squinted her eyes, and yanked her arm away, all at the same time. She rushed forward, tailgating Ashley down the staircase.

JUST AS BOB SAID AMEN, the phone rang. Everyone looked at Emily, who sat closest to it.

"What?" she said, her face reddening.

"The phone," Christopher said.

"Let it ring," Bob commanded.

Charlotte pushed her chair back. "It might be Dana." She stood. "Pete, I forgot to tell you she called earlier. About the tuxes."

As Charlotte excused herself, Emily turned to Pete. "Can I go with you to Harding tomorrow? I need more fabric for the dresses."

"Huh?" Pete squinted.

Charlotte was right. It was Dana, and she sounded even more stressed than before. When Charlotte mentioned seeing Bonnie and Grandma Maxie at lunch, Dana quickly changed the subject. Charlotte handed the phone off to Pete, who escaped into the family room with it.

As Charlotte passed the pot roast to Ashley, she strained her neck to catch Emily's gaze. "I don't think you should go tomorrow, sweetie, because of the dresses."

"Grandma," she wailed. "I'm going to need more fabric right away."

Pete hung up the phone. "I'm going tomorrow." He

pointed at Sam and then at Christopher. "So are the two of you." He had a sheepish look on his face.

"Wait until she hears what I did to one of the dresses," Ashley said.

"She's not going to hear about it." Emily practically yanked the basket of rolls from Ashley's hands. "Nobody says a word to Miss Simons." She looked around the table. "Got it?"

Christopher nodded.

"What'd you do?" Sam asked, a smirk on his face.

"I didn't do anything."

"Emily." Charlotte tried to catch her granddaughter's gaze. "That's enough."

Sam put his fork down. "Chill."

"Both of you stop. Now." Charlotte's voice was low and firm, perfectly controlled, hiding her anger, or so she thought. The children must have sensed it though because neither of them said a word. In fact everyone was silent for a moment, and Charlotte turned toward Ashley. "Do you want me to give you a ride home after dinner?"

She shook her head. "Mom's coming at eight. I'll help Emily until then."

Charlotte nodded. Ashley was such a good friend. She could hardly stand to see Emily take her for granted.

Bob cleared his throat. "Pete, do you plan to go window shopping again when you're in Harding?"

Pete shrugged, took another bite of roast, and then made an obvious attempt to change the subject. "So what's going on with the dresses?" he asked nonchalantly.

"Nothing," Emily barked. "As long as I go into Harding tomorrow."

Chapter Six

Emily positioned the screen for the T-shirt over the white fabric. She'd decided to do *bride* and *groom* shirts for Uncle Pete and Miss Simons as her silkscreening project in art class. Ms. Carey had started the class on a textile unit, beginning with screening. Emily was trying to ignore Ashley, but her friend kept talking.

"I just think we should be honest. I feel bad for deceiving Miss Simons the other day."

Emily leaned her hand against the tabletop. "For doing what?"

"Being deceptive. When we were talking about the dresses and I said we were talking about an art project."

"Oh, that." Emily moved the word *bride* a little to the right. She'd used simple, lowercase block letters with no embellishments for the words. Uncle Pete and Miss Simons could wear the T-shirts, which she'd found at Brenda's boutique for three dollars each, to the rehearsal. She'd thought up the project before they'd met with Bonnie Simons, and now she wondered if the woman would approve. She seemed to have pretty high expectations, which seemed surprising since Miss Simons wasn't a glamour girl or even that into fashion. But lately it seemed like she was getting pretty demanding too.

"I feel like I lied to her," Ashley said.

Emily looked at her and blinked.

"About the dresses." Ashley seemed annoyed.

"Oh, that," Emily said again. Boy, Ashley had a one-track mind today. "Well, you didn't lie. We do have an art project to work on. And besides, it was for her own good. If she'd known I hadn't even cut out all the dresses, she would have way overreacted. So would her mom; she's really into drama. So you did us all a favor."

Ashley shook her head. "I don't think so. Do you remember that talk at youth group about truth and honesty?"

Emily tilted her head. "No."

"It was last week, Emily." Ashley flipped her red curls over her shoulder. "We memorized the verse from Psalms, about God desiring truth from us."

Picking up the can of paint, Emily focused on the screen again. "Could we talk about this later? Please? I need to concentrate." Emily vaguely remembered the verse, something about being honest leading to wisdom, but Ashley was beating a dead horse, as Grandpa would say. The longer Emily put her off the better. Otherwise she would probably go running to Mrs. Simons for no good reason.

"When would be a good time to talk? After school?"

Emily shook her head as she sprayed the black paint back and forth across the screen. "I'm going to go to Harding with Uncle Pete." Emily removed the screen. Not bad. None of the letters had blurred. Now it was time to do Uncle Pete's *groom* shirt.

"Let's talk tomorrow, okay?" Ashley walked back to her seat at the front table as Emily let out a sigh.

"OVER HERE," Uncle Pete called from Grandma's Ford Focus. "We're taking the slowmobile into Harding."

Emily tramped across the slush-covered parking lot. The temperature had risen during the day, and the snow was melting. "Good riddance" was all she could say. It was high time for spring to arrive.

Christopher shuffled through the slush as he walked, a smile on his face.

"Shotgun!" Emily called out just as Sam flew down the steps to the high school. She plopped onto the front seat before Sam reached the parking lot.

Christopher's face fell. "Then I get it on the way home."

"Probably not," Emily said. "Did you forget Sam's coming?"

"Hurry up," Uncle Pete said. "'Cause, speaking of home, I'd like to get back sooner rather than later."

As Christopher climbed into the backseat, Uncle Pete kept talking. "I should spend some time with Dana tonight—since we are getting married in just over three weeks." He started the car. "Hey, where did Sam go?"

Emily squinted against the sun. Sam stood at the edge of the parking lot, talking to Arielle. His hands were shoved in the front pockets of his jeans, bunching up his coat, and he had that silly look on his face.

There was no way Arielle was going to get back together with him. She thought he was a loser, and the sooner he accepted that fact, the better.

Uncle Pete rolled forward and opened his window. "Hey, are you coming with us or not?"

Sam flashed a thumbs-up sign. Emily rolled her eyes.

Arielle took a step toward the car. "Sam was just telling me about the new calf."

Uncle Pete leaned out the window. "You should come see it one of these days."

Arielle looked at Sam, who gave a quick nod, and then back at Uncle Pete. "That would be fun."

Emily slunk down in the seat. *Yeah, right.* There was no way Arielle would be coming out to the farm again.

The car behind them honked, and Uncle Pete waved good-bye to Arielle. "Come on," he said to Sam, and then started humming the tune to "Matchmaker, Matchmaker."

"Would you stop?" Emily groaned.

"What?"

"Humming," Emily said as Sam slammed the back passenger door.

A minute later they were headed down the highway. A semi zoomed by them in the other lane, plastering a layer of slush over the car. Uncle Pete turned on the wipers and then the radio. Emily took out the swatch of fabric for the dresses. Hopefully they had more of the same fabric at the shop. She still couldn't believe how Ashley had messed things up.

EMILY SAT DOWN on a bench in Tuxes for You, wiggling in between Christopher and Sam. They'd waited for a half hour to be helped, and now it was taking forever. Uncle Pete stood with his arms spread out, turning his head toward the door of a fitting room, where a tux with a royal blue bow tie hung from a hook.

"That's just an example, right?" he asked as the salesman measured his arms.

"I double-checked the order just a minute ago." The man's voice was low and polite. He wore a white dress shirt and a paisley bow tie and cummerbund. "It's the right tux." He seemed to be moving in slow motion.

"I want a black tie," Uncle Pete said. "None of that bright stuff."

The man stepped away to the desk and came back with a form. "Dana Simons. March twenty-eighth wedding in Bedford. Right?"

Uncle Pete nodded.

"Five tuxes. All with royal blue ties and cummerbunds."

"Cumberwhats?" Uncle Pete asked.

Emily stood. "It's that thing that goes around your waist. And the blue looks really nice. It matches the dresses perfectly."

"No." Uncle Pete put his arms down. "Black matches the blue perfectly."

The salesman handed him the form. "I make it a practice not to get between a bride and the tuxes. Perhaps you would like to call your beloved?" He ran his fingers through his perfectly feathered hair.

Uncle Pete looked like he wanted to crumple the order form. "Hey, Em. Do you have your cell?"

Emily dug it out of her pocket and handed it to him as Christopher stood and walked to the front of the shop. Sam jumped to his feet and followed.

Uncle Pete stepped toward the dressing rooms, and

Emily stayed where she was, hoping she could hear the conversation.

"Hey, I'm at the tux shop, but the order got mixed up." He fingered the hem of the tux sleeve as he spoke. "I wanted black."

He was silent for a long stretch and then he finally said, "I definitely did not agree to any colors. I would remember that." Emily caught a view of his profile. His face was red. There was another pause and then, "No, I do remember saying I'd be fine with whatever you decided. But I thought you meant anything black." The next pause was short.

"So now you're okay with whatever I decide? And what about your mom?" There was another long pause and then, "So I probably will hear about this later?" And then, "I'll take my chances." A second later Uncle Pete handed the phone back to Emily without looking at her.

"Have we come to a decision?" the salesman asked.

"Not yet." Uncle Pete turned toward the front of the shop. "Hey, Christopher and Sam. Do you want black ties or bright blue ones?"

Christopher shrugged.

"It doesn't matter," Sam called out.

"Your best man and the other groomsman have already been in," the salesperson said. "They didn't complain."

Uncle Pete was silent for a moment and then said, "Okay, write this down. The groom gets black—everyone else gets the bright blue tie and that other thing."

"Royal blue," the man corrected. "And it's a cummerbund."

"Whatever," Uncle Pete muttered.

A half hour later, Emily urged Uncle Pete to drive faster

through downtown Harding. The fabric store was in a strip mall on the edge of town, and it closed at five. "Hurry," she said. They should have gone to the fabric store first.

Uncle Pete turned into the parking lot at 4:55, and as he pulled into a space in front of the store, Emily jumped from the car and slid on the sidewalk a little as she dashed toward the door. The temperature had plunged again and everything was icing over. She pushed through the double doors of the shop.

"We're closing," came a voice from the back.

"I'll be quick," Emily said, darting to the bridal corner in the back of the store as she pulled the swatch of fabric from her pocket. There was the fabric, in the same place as when she and Grandma had purchased the first batch a couple of weeks ago.

The sales clerk stood at the edge of the bridal area. "I said we're closing."

"I just need to buy a yard of this." Emily held the bolt in her arms.

The woman didn't budge.

"I've come all the way from Bedford."

"I remember you," the woman said and turned toward the front of the store. Emily followed as the bell to the front door buzzed and Uncle Pete, Sam, and Christopher entered.

"I need a yard more of this," Emily said, holding out her swatch. "My friend cut a sleeve out wrong."

"You're making bridesmaids' dresses, right?" The woman took the bolt of fabric and began uncoiling it onto the counter.

"Yep," Emily said as the swatch of fabric fell onto the counter.

"I can't guarantee that this bolt is from the same dye lot."

"Pardon?" It looked like the bolt and swatch were the same color.

"There can be minor variances in color." The woman measured off a yard.

"Will that make a difference?"

"It could. That's why we always advise people to buy extra fabric."

Emily wadded the swatch in her hand. "I did—over a yard extra."

"Then one sleeve isn't the only thing that you cut out wrong."

Emily ignored the woman. "I hope it's the same bolt of fabric."

"Oh, it's not," the woman said. "I just sold the rest of that original bolt to a woman from River Bend."

Uncle Pete hooted. "I wonder if Anna is making a blue dress to wear to the wedding."

"Oh, that would be awful," Emily said. How embarrassing that would be for all of them, but the chance of that was next to nothing. Surely it was some other woman in River Bend.

"Can you make the dress without sleeves?" The clerk asked. Emily shook her head. If she could, her life would be so much easier right now. That was why it had taken her so long to get started on the dresses—all the e-mails between the bridesmaids and Miss Simons about sleeves had set Emily back.

The clerk slipped the fabric into a bag. "That will be fifteen ninety-nine."

Uncle Pete hooted again. "For that little piece of fabric?"

"Just pay," Emily said, taking the package and starting out to the car.

Uncle Pete insisted on stopping at the tool store to show them the new tractor he'd been researching. They gathered around the monstrosity under the carport-like structure adjoining the store. "It's a John Deere, of course," Uncle Pete said, climbing up to the cab. Sam and Christopher climbed up behind him. "With a command center," he called out.

"And a touch screen," Christopher said.

Emily stepped away from the tractor. The little sign on the stand read MODEL 8230, 225 HP ENGINE, FUEL-EFFICIENT, $155,000. Emily gasped. That was as much as some houses—not in San Diego maybe, but around here. Uncle Pete was crazy.

"We should get going," Emily said. No wonder Grandpa didn't want Uncle Pete to go window-shopping.

BY THE TIME they started home, Christopher was complaining about being hungry.

"Shhh." Emily sat beside him in the backseat. "We'll be home in no time. Grandma will keep dinner warm for us."

Uncle Pete turned onto the highway. "Watch the landscape. Or go to sleep," Emily said, thinking she sounded like Grandma. "That will keep your mind off food." It wouldn't be long before the stars came out in the clear, night sky.

Uncle Pete turned up the heat. "Does it feel cold in here to you?" he asked.

Sam said, "A little bit."

Emily felt her window. It was freezing. It felt like the icy night was seeping through.

"Has Mom been having problems with her heater?" Uncle Pete asked.

Emily said she didn't think so.

"Maybe it's the thermostat. The gauge is leaning toward the cold side." Uncle Pete slowed for a curve. "Dad better check it tomorrow."

Emily leaned her head back and closed her eyes. Hopefully this yard of fabric would match the others. She couldn't imagine they'd be that different, even if they were from different bolts.

Uncle Pete began to brake. "Uh-oh."

Emily's eyes flew open. Ahead of them was a big bull, smack in the middle of the highway.

Uncle Pete pumped the brakes again and swerved into the other lane. Thank goodness there wasn't any traffic coming their way. Emily stiffened against the seat. The bull was just a few yards ahead, and as he raised his head the lights of the car caught his wild eyes. Suddenly he began charging toward the car. Emily didn't need to know geometry to know what was going to happen unless the bull stopped or Uncle Pete swerved again.

Jerking the steering wheel, Uncle Pete missed the bull, but the car went into a spin. Before Emily could scream or yell, the car had come to a stop, headed in the wrong direction but still on the road.

"Everyone okay?" Uncle Pete asked as he checked his rearview mirror. The bull turned his head toward them.

"I think so," Emily said. The bull lumbered to the other side of the highway and disappeared.

"What happened?" Christopher's voice was groggy.

"Uncle Pete missed a bull," Sam said.

Uncle Pete swung the car around and accelerated. "Standing in the middle of the highway."

"It's freezing in here," Christopher said.

Emily leaned over and put her arm around him. "We'll be home pretty soon."

"Tell Grandma she needs a new thermostat." Uncle Pete gripped the steering wheel.

Emily peered at the speedometer. He was only going forty-five, and his knuckles were white.

Chapter Seven

"Sounds like your uncle should have been driving more carefully—not doing whatever it was he was doing." Bob sat at the table, a bowl of apple cobbler in front of him. Pete had hurried to the upstairs landing to call Dana as soon as they'd arrived at the farm, leaving the children to tell about the trip home from Harding.

Charlotte wrapped her hands around her cup of decaf, breathing a prayer of thanks that everyone was all right.

"It wasn't Uncle Pete's fault." Emily held a paper bag close to her side.

"The bull was really big," Sam added.

"What matters is that you're all okay," Charlotte said, standing and putting her arm around Christopher.

"I didn't see it." Christopher spoke softly. "I was asleep."

Charlotte squeezed his shoulder and then said, "Go get washed up, all of you. The stew is still hot."

The boys headed down the hall, but Emily turned toward her grandmother. "I still have homework to do—and the sewing tonight."

"I'll call Aunt Rosemary in the morning—I know she'll help you." Charlotte turned toward the stove.

"Don't. Please. I can do it. I'm just tired today."

Five minutes later the children and Pete joined Bob at the table.

"Did you find more fabric?" Charlotte asked Emily.

Emily nodded but didn't offer any more information.

"How'd things go at the tux shop?" Charlotte asked Pete.

"Fine."

"Did you go anywhere else?" Charlotte passed the baking-soda biscuits to Sam.

"Just that tractor shop," Emily answered

Bob sat up straight. "Give it up, Pete. We can't afford a new tractor."

"I know, Dad." Pete had that old tone in his voice, one Charlotte hadn't heard for several years. "I'm just looking."

"But why? If we can't afford it, we can't afford it. And it made you late starting back—put you at risk for an accident."

Pete crossed his arms. "That's the most ridiculous thing I've ever heard. There was a bull in the road."

"The temperature was dropping. You should have left Harding earlier."

"Dad, nothing happened," Pete huffed.

Charlotte decided to change the subject. "The calf was doing well this afternoon," she said. "I gave him his bottles and the little guy was perky. The electrolytes must be working."

Sam smiled, but neither Bob nor Pete responded.

"And we had two more births out in the field. The mother cows and calves are all fine."

Pete nodded his head but still didn't answer. He shoved a spoonful of stew into his mouth.

Charlotte stood and put the pot of stew back on the stove. Why did she try? Bob and Pete would have to work out their own stuff, but the tension was getting to her. Something more than Pete's behavior was bugging Bob because, to be honest, Pete had been acting more and more responsibly over the last few years.

"By the way," Pete said, "something's wrong with Mom's car. It was freezing the whole way home."

Bob grunted.

Charlotte tried to ignore them both. Families were such fragile systems. It didn't take much to upset the balance, to put everyone on edge. A wedding. A near accident. Three unsewn dresses. A sick calf. Three motherless children. Life was full of uncertainty.

"I CAN'T SLEEP." Christopher stood in the doorway to the family room.

"It's because you slept on the way home from Harding," Charlotte said. "Go read for a while." She sat at her desk, sorting through the bills. She was too tired to pay them tonight, but she wanted to have a head start in the morning.

"Can you come tuck me in?" Christopher stood on one leg, rubbing his shin with the other.

"I already did."

"Again."

Charlotte raised her head and looked straight at her grandson. "Go back up to bed. I'll come check on you in a little bit." Christopher retreated up the stairs as a feeling of regret crept over Charlotte. Did she not have enough time to cater to him just a little? What if tonight's near miss had caused him to think again about his mother's fatal accident?

A few minutes later Charlotte pushed back from the desk and headed upstairs. She knocked on Christopher's door.

"Come in." His voice was so low she could barely make it out.

His light was off. Charlotte sat down on the side of the bed and found his face by the light of the moon coming through the window. "You okay, sweetie?"

He shook his head.

"What's the matter?"

He took a deep breath. "Do I have to wear a tux?"

Charlotte, in her relief, couldn't help but smile.

"It's not funny, Grandma. Why can't I wear my own clothes?" he whined.

"It's what Miss Simons wants. And when a bride wants something, we do our best to accommodate her."

"Uncle Pete doesn't."

"Pardon?"

"Uncle Pete doesn't accommodate Miss Simons. She ordered a blue tie, and he changed his to black."

"Oh." Charlotte pushed Christopher's sweaty hair away from his face. "Well, your uncle Pete's the groom so he gets some say. The rest of us do what we can to give them what they want."

Christopher rolled on his side, away from Charlotte. "All anyone thinks about around here is that wedding," he muttered.

Charlotte patted his back. "What else should we be thinking about?" As she said the words she knew. "Besides your birthday."

Christopher rolled back toward her. "I thought you'd forgotten."

"Of course I haven't forgotten." She tousled his hair again. "Weddings are important—but so are birthdays."

Christopher nodded and then he said, "I just want a family birthday—something simple." He smiled, just a little, and Charlotte kissed his forehead.

"Sweet dreams," she whispered and then slipped out of the room.

"IT JUST FEELS LIKE something else is going on," Charlotte said as she pulled on her pajamas, still annoyed with Bob's earlier surliness toward Pete.

"Because I chastised Pete for almost wrecking your car?" Bob was already tucked into bed, the down comforter pulled up to his chin, his whiskered face shadowed in the dim light of the lamp.

"It seems more than that." Charlotte pulled a pair of warm footies from her dresser drawer and sat on the edge of the bed, her back to Bob, and slipped the socks onto her feet. It felt like January again.

Bob didn't answer, and she searched his face as she crawled under the covers. "What's up?" she asked.

Bob's eyes looked heavy, but he turned his head toward her slightly. "It's his judgment. Why is he shopping for a tractor when we can't afford it? And what other harebrained decisions is he going to be making about the farm?" Bob yawned and then said, "What if he decides to buy that tractor?"

Charlotte scooted closer to Bob, seeking the warmth of his body. "He can't. Not without you signing for it too."

"Well, thank goodness for that," Bob said. He sighed. "How old is Pete? Thirty?"

"Thirty-four," Charlotte answered.

"He still acts like a kid. It's hard to imagine him married, let alone in charge of the farm."

"Sweetheart, everyone makes mistakes." She could remember mistakes Bob had made back when they were first married. One year he didn't plant enough alfalfa for the cows and didn't buy enough either. He ended up paying top dollar in February to get his herd through the winter.

Bob reached over and turned off the lamp, and Charlotte knew he was done talking for the night.

Why did Bob still treat Pete like a kid? Was it because of Pete's personality? Or because he was the last-born child? Or because Bob couldn't remember what it was like to be young anymore?

Chapter Eight

Sam woke to the steady beat of water pelting the flower bed below his window. It was still dark outside as he made out the blurry numbers 5:15 on his alarm clock. He closed his eyes again, thinking that forty-five minutes of sleep sounded like a really good thing, but the drumming of the melting snow made his heart beat faster. He swung his feet over the edge of his bed. He might as well get up and feed Snowflake his morning bottle. Poor thing was probably pretty lonely out there in the barn.

He padded down to the kitchen, and as he mixed the calf starter with warm water, Grandpa wandered in wearing his old-man pajamas. It took a moment for his grandfather to see Sam, and when he did he startled.

"What are you doing up so early?" Grandpa fiddled with the switch on the coffeemaker as he spoke.

"I thought I'd go ahead and give the calf his bottle." Sam reached over and flipped the switch, and immediately the machine began to sputter. Grandma must have set it up before she went to bed last night.

As he slid onto a kitchen chair, Grandpa asked if Pete was up.

"I don't think so," Sam answered, shaking the bottle, his finger over the latex nipple as the scent of coffee filled the room.

Grandpa shook his head.

"Why are you up so early?" Sam asked.

"The weather woke me. You can tell it's nearly spring—one minute it's freezing, and the next it's thawing. Got me thinking about planting and all the work that needs to be done around here."

Sam grinned. "Me too."

Grandpa straightened his back. "You too? Since when do you think about the farm?"

Sam shrugged. "Well, I'm thinking about the calf; that's for sure."

Grandpa nodded and then stood and took the cream out of the fridge and a cup out of the cupboard, placing them both alongside the coffeemaker. Sam left him staring at the hissing, burbling appliance.

The thaw was in full force as Sam stepped out the back door. The snow was already slushy under his feet and had melted halfway down the barn and shop roofs, and off the top of his car. He increased his stride. He'd be able to drive to school today, he was sure, and that meant he could drive home too, and maybe ask Arielle to come out to the farm with him after school. She'd said that she wanted to see the calf—and it really seemed like she did.

He wondered if he should ask her during first period or wait until later, to give her less time to think about it. If he asked her early in the day, she might say yes and then change her mind. For a second he wondered if it was worth asking her at all. She could be so moody. He didn't miss that about her, but he did miss talking with her, hearing what she thought about things. He missed having her listen to him.

He pushed open the barn door. "Hey, buddy," he called out. "It's breakfast time."

By the time he reached the pen Snowflake was on his feet and bawling.

"Hey, little guy," Sam cooed. "Here's your milk."

The calf butted his head against Sam's leg and then connected with the bottle, jerking on it as he sucked. Sam held on tight. Snowflake was getting stronger; he downed the bottle in record time and started butting his head against Sam's leg.

"Whoa, buddy," Sam said, backing out of the pen and closing the gate behind him. He grabbed the jug of electrolytes off the shelf and filled the bottle with the clear liquid. "I've got a little something more for you."

A minute later Snowflake finished off the second bottle and started nuzzling Sam's leg again.

"That's it," Sam said, petting the calf's head. "Sorry if it wasn't enough." He grabbed the pitchfork and lifted the soiled straw from around Snowflake. Then he eased his way through the gate, dropping the load into the wheelbarrow. He repeated the process two more times and then spread fresh straw, all the while dodging Snowflake. When Sam stepped out for the final time and started toward the barn door, the calf began to bawl again.

"Ahh," Sam said, returning to the gate. Snowflake looked up at him with his big brown eyes, still begging, his little pink tongue at the edge of his mouth. "You just want more milk."

The calf pawed at the gate.

"Or maybe you just want me." Sam reached through the slats and scratched the top of Snowflake's head. "But I have to go to school. I'll see you this after..."

Sam's words trailed off. He was talking to an animal. He raised his hand in a wave and then hurried out the barn door and across the slushy driveway, followed by Snowflake's complaints.

He heard voices as he swung open the back door.

"Dad, you're blowing this out of proportion." It was Uncle Pete. Next, Sam heard him say, "Who's up already?"

"Sam," Grandpa said. "He's turning into a farmer after all."

Sam stepped into the kitchen. "Hi," he said.

Uncle Pete wore jeans and a sweatshirt. "How's the weather out there?"

"Great. I thought I'd drive to school today." Sam didn't like coffee, but sitting around the table drinking it with his uncle and grandfather looked appealing. Instead he took the pitcher of milk from the fridge and filled a glass and then sat down, aware of the awkward silence between the two men.

Uncle Pete set his cup down firmly. "I'm only looking at a tractor."

Grandpa nodded. "But I told you to stop."

Uncle Pete's face was bright red.

Grandpa didn't say anything more, but Grandma's voice came from the hall. "Please, you two, could you talk about something else?" She appeared in her bathrobe, her hair all scrunched to the side, like Christopher's when he first woke up. "Oh, Sam," she said. "Have you already fed the calf?"

Sam nodded. "I gave him one bottle of milk and one of electrolytes. But he still acted hungry. He cried and cried when I left."

His uncle smiled, just a little. "I should try to graft him to another cow today."

"Could you wait until after school—until I get home?" Sam's face felt warm.

Uncle Pete pushed his chair back. "Why?"

Sam fidgeted with the base of his glass. "I'd like to give him one last bottle, that's all."

Uncle Pete pulled his hat onto his head. "We'll see. Who knows? If the cow won't take him you'll still have a job."

Nodding, Grandma poured cream into a cup. "I think Snowflake thinks you're his mama," Grandma said. "I think it's more likely that Snowflake will be the one who won't cooperate, don't you think, Pete?" Grandma turned around.

But Grandpa, crossing his arms, didn't seem to find any of it amusing. "He'd better graft onto a cow. We can't afford to keep giving him the calf starter."

STUDENTS FILLED THE HALLS after second period, pushing and jostling each other, opening lockers and slamming them shut again. Sam hurried by his friend Jake.

"Hey, where's the fire?" Jake called after him.

Sam waved and headed for the sociology room, peering through the door. No Arielle. He stepped to the left of the door, his eyes on the bulletin board. The Future Farmers of America were having a carnival in a couple of weeks. That looked like fun. March 28. Maybe he could ask Arielle. He rubbed the side of his face. The date seemed familiar. Oh, yeah, it was Uncle Pete's wedding.

"Hey." Arielle stopped beside him. Her dark hair was pulled back, and she wore a blue sweatshirt that made her eyes extra bright.

"Hey," he responded.

"What are you looking at?"

Sam shoved his sweaty hands into the pockets of his jeans. "The FFA carnival—but I'm busy that night."

"Oh." Arielle started toward the door. "How's the calf?"

"Good. Want to come out and see it after school?" He grimaced. He hadn't meant to blurt out his invitation like that.

"Maybe," Arielle said. And then she smiled that killer smile.

"Do you have to work today?" he asked.

She shook her head. "I'll let you know this afternoon." She stepped ahead of him and sat down at her desk.

Sam shuffled a few rows back and slid into his seat.

"Hey," Jake said, sauntering into the room. "There you are. What's wrong with you?" He slapped Sam's shoulder.

"Nothin'," Sam muttered and then sighed. He wished he hadn't asked Arielle out to the farm at all. Now he'd spend the rest of the day agonizing over what her answer would be.

SHE WAS MESSING with him; he was sure. She hadn't said anything at lunch. He wasn't going to beg. He had snuck out of last period early and went to his locker. Now he slammed it shut, hearing the clang of the metal against metal as he stepped into the middle of the hall as the last bell rang. He turned toward the front door. He'd wait in his car for Emily.

He'd reached the bottom of the front steps when he heard his name. He turned quickly.

"Sam!" It was Arielle. She stopped on the top step. "Were you going to wait for me?"

"I didn't think you were coming."

"You didn't wait for my answer." Arielle held tightly onto her book bag.

"Sorry," Sam said. He nodded toward the parking lot. "Come on."

"Can you give me a ride back into town after I see the calf?" she asked as they made their way through the slush toward the car.

"Sure." He tried to think of something more to say but nothing came to mind.

As he opened the passenger door for her, Christopher came bustling around the side of the car.

"Oh," he said. And then to Arielle, "Hi."

"Get in on my side, okay?" Sam said to his brother and then shut Arielle's door. He was hoping that Christopher would be talkative, but he seemed just as tongue-tied as Sam was as he jumped over a puddle and made his way around the car.

"Guess I get the front seat," Emily called out as she tiptoed through the slush and water.

"Guess again," Sam said.

"You're not giving Jake a ride are you?" She stomped the last few steps, sending up sprays of water.

"No, Arielle."

"Arielle!" Emily's voice carried across the parking lot.

Sam frowned at her.

As Emily ducked into the backseat, she said, "Hi, there," to Arielle.

Turning toward the car, Sam stole a look at Arielle. She was talking to Emily. "I wanted to see the calf."

"Oh, he'll probably be out in the field by the time we get home." Emily spoke in her know-it-all voice. "Uncle Pete was going to pawn him off on some cow."

"Really?" Now Arielle was looking at Sam.

"It's called 'grafting,' Em, but he was going to wait to do that," Sam said, backing out of the parking spot. "Until tonight."

"Well, when I went out to feed the chickens, right before we left, he was talking about it. He had the cow in the corral."

Sam shot Emily a stop-talking look in the rearview mirror.

GRANDMA SAT AT THE TABLE with one of those women's magazines with recipes as Sam led the way into the kitchen.

"Oh hi, Arielle," she said. "What a nice surprise." Then she smiled at Sam.

At least Grandma remembered how to be polite.

"Hello, Mrs. Stevenson." Arielle seemed to relax a little.

"What brings you out to the farm?" Grandma stood.

"She wants to see the baby calf," Emily said. "But didn't Pete already take it out of the barn?"

"I don't think so." Grandma pulled an apple out of the fruit bowl and began washing it. "He's been seeding all day. He didn't even come in for lunch—not even to check to see if he had any phone messages." Grandma pulled a knife from the block. "Sam, put some cookies on a plate."

"I want to go see Snowflake before we have a snack." Sam peeled the lid off a new container of calf formula. "How about you, Arielle?"

"Sure," she said, and then added, to Grandma, "and then a snack would be great. Before Sam takes me home."

Sam filled the bottle with powder and water and then shook the warm liquid thoroughly. Thank goodness Uncle Pete hadn't moved the calf yet. The afternoon was starting to look a little better.

Five minutes later, they stood in front of an empty pen in the barn.

"Ah, Uncle Pete," Sam said, clutching the bottle, unable to hide his disappointment.

"It's okay." Arielle kicked at the straw on the barn floor. "We can go see him in the field."

Sam led the way, feeling choked up, the bottle still warm in his hand, a little surprised at how sad he felt. They slipped through the tack room and out the side door and then picked their way through the slush and mud. Arielle wore suede boots, but she wasn't making a big deal about it. Sam liked that about her. She didn't whine.

The afternoon sun was waning, but it had done a good

day's work, ridding the farm of the snow and ice. As they turned the corner around the far side of the barn, Uncle Pete's voice echoed past them. "Hey!" he bellowed.

Sam hurried his steps. Uncle Pete was in the corral, chasing Snowflake around an old cow. Uncle Pete lunged, reaching for Snowflake, but the calf faked to the right and Uncle Pete slid in the mud, going down on one hand and doing a half spin.

Arielle giggled. "Oh, what a cute calf!"

Climbing up on the fence, Sam yelled, "What's up?" and as soon as Snowflake heard his voice, he spun around, tearing across the corral to the fence, his black face tilted up, his eyes bright, stopping in front of Sam. He began to bawl.

Uncle Pete stood, wiping his muddy hand on the back of his jeans. "Hey, get that bottle out of here."

Sam hid it behind his coat.

Snowflake bawled again and then pressed his nose against Sam's leg.

"He's so cute," Arielle said.

Sam climbed down and rubbed the calf's white spot on his head through the slats, calling out to Uncle Pete, "You said you'd wait until after school."

"I did." Uncle Pete walked toward them.

"I wanted to give him one last bottle."

"He has to be hungry—otherwise he won't graft." Uncle Pete stopped by the calf. "But it's obvious to me now that you can't be around either." He smirked. "The little guy thinks you're his mama."

Sam raised his head, bumping it on the fence. "No, he doesn't."

"Of course he does." Uncle Pete sighed. "It's kind of funny—but kind of not funny too."

Snowflake began licking Sam's pant leg, and Sam tried to pat him away, but the calf started nibbling at Sam's fingers.

"Might as well give him the bottle," Uncle Pete said.

"Back in the pen?"

"Sure." Uncle Pete opened the gate.

"Come on, Snowflake," Sam said, walking along the fence, the calf following until he scurried through the gate, through the door into the tack room, and back into the barn, staying just inches behind Sam.

"He's like a dog," Arielle said.

"He's gotten so much stronger in just a few days." Sam opened the gate to the pen, but Snowflake wouldn't go in until Sam entered first.

As Sam took the bottle from the pocket of his coat, Snowflake let out a cry and lunged for it. After a second, Sam asked Arielle if she wanted to hold the bottle.

"Of course," she said, taking over. She giggled as Snowflake butted his head and yanked on the bottle as if he could make it flow faster. "This is so cool."

Sam knew exactly what she meant.

"Why does your uncle want to make him nurse from another cow? Why don't you just keep giving him a bottle?" Arielle asked, settling down on the bale of hay, keeping her hand steady.

"Grandpa's worried about money or something." It seemed like Grandpa was always worried about money. How much could calf starter cost—it was just powdered milk.

When Snowflake had drained the bottle, he butted against Arielle's leg.

"OK, take the bottle away," Sam said, grabbing the calf.

"He's still hungry."

"So he thinks. Now we give him a bottle of this electrolyte stuff."

Arielle stepped out of the pen with him. "That's for babies," she said as Sam filled the bottle. "It *is* expensive—we sell it at the pharmacy."

"Snowflake was sick. This has helped his tummy troubles."

"You know, baby formula is expensive too. Your grandfather probably has a point."

Sam shrugged.

"And who gets up with him in the night?"

"I do," Sam said. Well, he had a couple of times. So had Grandma.

"Really?"

Sam nodded.

"I'm impressed," she said, taking the bottle from him.

"THANK YOU," Arielle said as she opened the passenger door of the car. "I had a great time."

"Sure." Sam hoped he sounded positive. "Want to come out again sometime?"

"Maybe." She climbed out of the car and then turned back toward him, bending down. "You're good with Snowflake."

"Thanks," he said.

She turned toward her house, slinging her book bag over her shoulder. The front door opened, and Mrs. Friesen stepped onto the porch. She squinted into the setting sun, and then, as if she had just realized who he was, waved.

Sam waved back before pulling out of their driveway and back onto the street, exhaling. That hadn't been so bad. Maybe Arielle didn't think he was a total loser after all. He turned onto the highway and left the city limits. A minute later a little red car zoomed by him. He looked down at his speedometer. He was going sixty.

The red car zipped around a curve and out of sight. Sam slapped the side of his head—it was Miss Simons. Maybe she was headed out to the farm to see Uncle Pete.

When Sam pulled around the curve, the red car was nearly out of sight.

Chapter Nine

Pete stopped his pickup beside the shop and turned off the motor. It had been a good day. He'd gotten the Home Quarter seeded with wheat and would start the North Quarter in the morning. The only thing he hadn't gotten done was grafting Snowflake to another cow. The old cow he'd chosen had been plenty cooperative. The calf was the problem. Well, Sam was the problem, to be exact. He shouldn't have let the calf get so attached to his nephew.

As he opened the door of the pickup, lights swung down the driveway toward the house. He hopped down. It was probably Sam; he must have taken Arielle home. Pete started toward the house; he'd worked straight through lunch and was famished. A horn honked and he turned. It wasn't Sam. It was Dana.

He waved. She was coming in pretty fast. He took a step backward as she slid to a stop in the gravel.

"Hey," he said, stepping around to her door, ready to open it, but it flew toward his face before he could reach for the handle.

"Pete Stevenson." Dana climbed from her car. She wore her school clothes, a skirt and blouse with a short trench-like coat and knee-high boots. Her dark hair flew around her face, falling from clips on each side. "Why didn't you return my message?"

Pete stumbled backward. "What message?"

"The one I left this morning. And don't tell me you didn't get it."

"Whoa. This is the first time all day I've been back to the house."

She put her hands on her hips. For half a second she looked like her mother.

"Well, I did get as close as the corral, trying to get the calf to nurse from another cow, but Sam messed that all up." Another set of lights turned into the driveway. "But no one told me you called." Pete wondered if Dana's mom's perfectionism was rubbing off on her.

"Pete." Dana stepped forward. "I haven't seen you for three days—we've hardly talked on the phone."

"Sweetheart—"

Her eyes flashed.

The sound of tires on gravel came toward them.

"Come in and get something to eat," Pete said. "I'm starving and you probably are too. Can we talk after that?"

"No." She dropped her arms to her sides. "I want to talk now."

Sam pulled his car in between them and the house, and then Sam's car door opened. "Hi, guys," he said. "How's it going?"

"Fine," Pete answered. Dana didn't say anything.

"Oh," Sam said, leaning toward the house. "Guess I'll see you inside."

Pete nodded. He and Dana stood in silence for a moment. Finally she sighed and said, "I guess maybe I should eat. I don't think I had lunch either. And I haven't been sleeping very well."

He reached for her hand, but she turned away from him. Dropping his, he led the way.

He took her coat when they reached the mud porch and hung it up over his, wondering just how mad she was at him and why. People joked about women getting all worked up about their weddings but he never expected it from Dana. He gestured for her to enter the kitchen first, but she shook her head. He led the way. "Mom," he yelled, "we have company."

Mom was headed toward the table, another plate and glass in her hands. "That's what Sam said. So good to see you, Dana."

Dana smiled.

"I hope you're hungry. We're having spareribs for dinner."

"Spareribs?" Pete said. "In March?"

"I know—we usually barbecue them, but once the snow started melting I got a hankering for summer. This was as close as I could get."

"I'll go wash up," Dana said, ducking toward the hall.

"Is everything okay?" Mom whispered.

Pete shrugged and then grimaced. "She's upset with me."

"She left a message this morning."

"That I didn't get—so I didn't return the call." Pete nabbed a carrot stick from the table. "That's why she's upset."

Mom elbowed him. "Go wash your hands."

Pete headed down the hall as he crunched the carrot.

The bathroom door was closed, so he decided to go to the upstairs bathroom. He looked down at his sweatshirt. He should probably put on a clean shirt while he was at it. Taking the stairs two at a time, he tried to remember if it really had been three days since he'd seen Dana.

He knew he'd seen her the day the calf was born. That was Sunday. And he had talked to her that night on the phone and the next night as well. Then he'd talked to her on the phone Tuesday from the tux shop and then later that night after they got home. Sure, he had thought he'd go see her that night, but then he was too tired after the dicey trip home.

He knew Dana's mom was getting on her nerves, but there wasn't anything Pete could do about that except to steer clear of both of them. He hadn't seen Dana last night or talked to her—at least he didn't think he had phoned her. The days were all running together.

The upstairs bathroom door was closed too, so he knocked on it.

"Just a minute," Emily said.

"Just a minute or just an hour?" Pete answered back.

Emily ignored him.

"Well, I hope it's a minute. It's time to eat, and I need to wash up." He headed down the hall to his room. He twisted out of his sweatshirt and then chose a blue long-sleeved T-shirt to wear.

What if this was the way Dana really was? Highstrung and overreactive? What if she turned out like her mom? Not the way she looked—he wouldn't mind if she put on some weight and got soft around the edges—but what if she was always a little mad, a little unhappy? That wasn't fair—Bonnie Simons didn't seem mad and unhappy. Just a little on edge. But she was that way all the time.

"You can wash up," Emily yelled.

"Dinner's on," Mom called up the stairs.

"I'll be right there." Pete headed into the bathroom. When he was done and opened the door he found Dana waiting on the landing.

"What took you so long?" she asked.

"Just washing up," he said.

"Everyone is waiting." She started down the stairs, her hips swinging a little, a bounce in her step.

He caught her arm at the bottom of the stairs. "Dana," he said. "Truce? At least while we eat?"

Her eyes filled with tears.

"Baby, what is it?" he asked.

She leaned her head against his chest. "I'm just so tired of planning this wedding and dealing with everything: my mom, the flowers." She took a ragged breath. "You."

DANA WAS QUIET all through dinner, only speaking when someone asked her a question. It wasn't until a rib got away from Pete, landed on his blue shirt, and then tumbled to the table that she volunteered a comment, saying, "You need a bib."

Sam began to chuckle.

"I used to wear a bib," Christopher said.

"We remember," Emily said as she cut her veggie patty into bites. "But you were a baby."

Pete leaned over and picked up the rib. "Yep, me and babies." He wrapped the bone in his napkin and tucked it under his plate. "Speaking of babies, Sam, I think I'll give that son of yours his bottle after dinner."

"No, I want to do it," Sam said.

"No." Pete wiped his hands on Christopher's napkin. "He's too bonded to you. We all need to take turns."

Sam wrinkled his nose.

"Listen to your uncle," Dad said. "If we're not careful, we'll spend more in calf formula than we'll make off the thing when we butcher him."

"Butcher him?" Sam sat up straight.

"Well, we're not going to keep him as a bull," Dad said. "Right, Pete?"

Pete nodded, hoping that would be the end of that conversation.

"I need to go home after dinner," Dana said. "I have a stack of papers to grade."

"Help me feed the calf first," Pete said, hoping he didn't sound like he was begging. That had been his whole plan all along, that they could talk in the barn, because it was obvious they couldn't talk in the house, not with everyone around.

Dana took a drink of water and caught his eyes over the rim of her glass. They still sparked with anger. So much for the truce. "All right," she said.

PETE OPENED THE GATE to Snowflake's pen, but the calf stood in the far corner and bawled. "He wants Sam." Pete laughed. "Poor little guy." He handed the bottle to Dana. "Maybe he'll take it from you."

Dana looked cute in his mom's brown corduroy coat,

which hung down to those funky boots she wore. It was funny how, when she dressed up, he really felt she was out of his league.

She took the bottle and held it out. "Like this?" she asked.

Pete nodded.

Snowflake took a step toward her and bawled again.

"Come on," she said. "It's okay."

The calf connected with the bottle and began to suck.

"See, you have the touch," Pete said. He leaned against the gate. "So what did you want to talk about?"

She twisted toward him, looking away from the calf. "Everything. How is Emily doing on the dresses? How can I survive my mother for three more weeks? And where have you been? You never return my calls."

"I'm right here—just a little busy is all." Pete crossed his arms. "And I'm sure Emily is doing fine on the dresses."

"I wasn't worried at first—I just figured she could handle it. But Ashley said something funny this morning, before school started."

Pete raised his eyebrows.

"Something about how she had been deceptive the other day, acting like Emily was further along than she was."

"Huh." Pete had no idea what was going on.

"Maybe you could talk to your mom. Maybe she could sit down with Emily and make a chart or something. At least that's what my mom suggested."

Pete nodded. "Okay." He reached out and patted Dana's arm. "And what about your mom?"

"She's determined that we should have roses for the wedding—because that's what she wanted but wasn't able to have."

"Roses sound okay."

"I want white tulips. I know roses are old-fashioned, but the tulips work with the dresses and with the photos on the program, at least as well as the roses do."

"Then tulips it is." Pete grinned. That was easy.

"She already ordered roses. She said she was certain that's what I wanted."

"Tell her to unorder them."

Snowflake jerked on the empty bottle, and Pete took it out of Dana's hands and headed out to fill it with water. It was time to stop the electrolytes, since the calf was about done with being handfed. Besides, it was all gone, and he didn't want to buy more. Pete walked to the far end of the barn, to the spigot that flowed into the trough for the horses. When he returned to the pen, Dana was sitting on a bale of hay and Snowflake was sniffing at her coat.

"Maybe roses would be all right," Dana said, looking up.

"They're fine with me." Pete handed her the bottle.

"Everything is fine with you, Pete," she said, thrusting the water toward the calf.

"I just want you to be happy," he said, tugging at his hat.

"No, you don't." She turned her head away. "You just want me to stop talking."

AFTER DANA LEFT, Pete stood by the back door, holding his mom's coat. It smelled like Dana, whatever that fragrance was that he could never remember. It smelled good, like sweet peas growing alongside the fields in the early summer. Or maybe it was like gardenias. He sighed.

It wasn't that he wanted her to stop talking, not really. He opened the back door. No. It *was* that he wanted her to stop talking. He didn't really care about the details of the wedding and there wasn't anything he could do about her mom. And he felt bad that maybe Emily was stressing Dana out about the dresses. Mostly he didn't want Dana to be stressed and unhappy. It wasn't like her.

He hung the coat on a hook on the mud porch and headed into the kitchen. Emily had her back turned to him, scraping leftovers into a container. The evening dessert was still on the table, a berry cobbler. He dished a big spoonful into a bowl and took a bite. It tasted like there was some rhubarb in it too.

Emily placed the container in the fridge and then noticed Pete. "Oh," she said. "Where'd you come from?"

"Telling Dana good-bye."

"How is she?" Emily asked as she grabbed the dishcloth and started wiping down the counters.

"Stressed."

"About?"

"The wedding. The dresses in particular."

Emily stopped at the end of the yellow counter and turned around. "Why?"

"It seems Ashley said you've hardly started." Pete took another bite of the cobbler.

"Ashley said that?" Emily tossed the dishcloth into the sink.

"Something like that."

Emily raked her hand through her hair, stopping at her ponytail holder. She frowned. "Well, that's not true."

Pete held up his fork. "That's great. You should tell Dana."

Emily shook her head. "Tell her not to worry. I have the dresses under control. Really," she said as she pranced out of the kitchen.

Pete finished his cobbler and put the dish on the counter. He yawned and glanced at the clock. 7:45. He felt as if it were midnight.

Chapter Ten

Saturday morning after breakfast, Emily sat on her bed and stared at the mounds of royal blue fabric that had overtaken her bedroom. Her dress was draped over the sewing machine, the front and back attached to each other and the sleeves basted into place. The sleeves still seemed a little off. Could she have cut them out wrong too? She shook her head. No. She'd been so careful. She still hadn't started Michelle's and Amber's dresses. And now Miss Simons was stressed.

"Emily?" It was Grandma at the door.

Emily hurried to her desk and sat down, positioning her dress in the sewing machine.

"Emily?" Grandma called out again.

"Come in."

"How is it going?" Grandma stepped over the pile of fabric in the middle of the room.

"Good."

Grandma had that look on her face. "I need you to be totally honest with me."

Emily nodded.

"Tell me exactly how far along you are with each dress." Grandma glanced down at the pile of cut pieces as she spoke.

Emily bowed her head. "This is all a lot harder than I thought." It was Amber's fault. She was the one who had insisted on sleeves, even if they were just cap sleeves.

Grandma stepped around the dress pieces and touched Emily on the shoulder. "What do you need, sweetie? What can I do to help?"

Emily raised her head. "I don't need any help. Really, I've got everything under control."

Grandma crossed her arms. "I'll check back in two hours and see how things are going."

After Grandma left, Emily ripped the basting stitches out and then repinned the fabric, carefully matching the pleats. Amber had said in an e-mail that someday Emily would understand, when she was in her thirties, about wanting sleeves. Emily basted the sleeve again and held it up. It still didn't look right. She grabbed the seam ripper again and jabbed at the thread, poking the fabric instead.

Later, when Grandma knocked on the door again, Emily was lying on her bed, staring at the ceiling. Grandma knocked a second time. "Come in," Emily said, sitting up.

As Grandma opened the door, Emily said, "I don't think we should bother Dana about the dresses, but do you think Aunt Rosemary would help—unless she feels bad that we didn't order the fabric from her?"

Grandma shook her head. "She wouldn't hold it against us, I'm sure."

Emily dangled her legs. "Can you ask her if I can go over to the shop today?" If she had to rip that sleeve off one more time she would probably destroy the whole dress.

Grandma headed toward the door. "I'll go call right now."

Emily picked up the pieces of Amber's dress and put them on the bed, folding them one by one. The dresses were consuming her life. She couldn't concentrate on her homework. She was avoiding Miss Simons in the halls—and now Ashley too. It was like the dresses were stalking her, marching relentlessly through her days and nights.

She shuddered. To think she had volunteered at first to make Miss Simons's wedding gown. She stacked the folded pieces and slipped them into a bag. At least with a wedding dress she would have had to make only one—not three. She groaned, unable to imagine what she was going to do if Aunt Rosemary couldn't help her.

After folding Michelle's dress pieces too, Emily shuffled out of her room and down the stairs toward Grandma's voice in the kitchen.

"Okay. I'll have Sam drop her off after school on Monday then. Bye."

"Monday," Emily wailed. "Why not today?"

"Well." Grandma hung up the phone. "Rosemary has agreed to help Anna sew the flower girl dresses. And help with a skirt for Anna too."

"Grandma!" Emily slumped into a chair. The flower girl dresses couldn't be that hard. And Aunt Anna had plenty of dresses that would work for the wedding already. "The bridesmaids' dresses should take priority. Don't you think?"

"Anna asked first. Rosemary is happy to help you on Monday though." Grandma sighed. "And I'd be happy to help you today."

Emily buried her head in her arms on the tabletop as the

phone rang. The phone stopped ringing, and then Grandma's perky voice rang out. "Oh, hi again, Rosemary."

Emily groaned.

"Oh, really," Grandma said. "Let me just double-check." She paused. "Sweetie?"

Emily raised her head.

"Rosemary just talked with Anna—she's too tired to make it today. Aunt Rosemary said to come on over. Is that still what you want?"

Emily stood. "Yes," she said. "Yes, please!" She hugged Grandma, her arms falling around her grandmother's middle. "Thank you, Aunt Rosemary!" she called out into the phone.

Grandma chuckled and then said, "Okay. We'll see you in a few."

"ASHLEY CUT THE SLEEVE on Amber's dress wrong." Emily pulled her sewing machine from its case as Aunt Rosemary surveyed the pieces of the dresses Grandma had unfolded on the table.

"Emily." Grandma dangled her car keys in her hand, ready to go.

"It's true. Ashley even said so."

Aunt Rosemary picked up Emily's dress, with the sleeve half basted to the bodice. "What happened here?"

Emily blushed. "I had a hard time sewing those on."

Holding the dress in front of her, the royal blue fabric cascading toward the floor, Aunt Rosemary chuckled and then said, "Sweetie, no wonder. This is cut wrong too."

"Oh, dear," Grandma said, stepping closer. "I didn't catch that."

Emily reached for the dress. "Is that why the notches wouldn't line up?"

"Yep. These sleeves are really tricky—but cute." Aunt Rosemary pulled a seam ripper from her pocket. "Charlotte?" She held out the little tool.

"Sure," Grandma said, putting down her keys. "I can help for a little while."

"Now, let's take a look at your extra fabric and see if we have enough—or if Dana will have to settle for sleeveless."

Emily held up the material. "I bought extra—on Tuesday." She handed it to Aunt Rosemary. "The lady said there might be some problems with the dye, but it looks fine to me."

Squinting, Rosemary held the fabric next to Amber's dress. "I don't know, sweetie. It looks a little off."

Emily groaned.

Aunt Rosemary smiled and Emily could tell she was teasing. "I think it's fine—even though you didn't buy the fabric from me."

Emily nodded, and Grandma gushed, "We've learned our lesson. Believe me."

"Well, we'll see if there's enough fabric or not," Aunt Rosemary said as the front door to the shop buzzed. "Why don't you get started sewing Michelle's front and back together?" she said, limping just a little as she walked.

"Is something wrong with her?" Emily whispered to Grandma.

"I don't think so. Maybe she's just tired."

Emily hoped that was all. She gathered the two biggest pieces to Michelle's dress and the pincushion from her sewing box. "Do you think I can come on Monday after school, even though Aunt Anna will be here?"

Grandma picked the thread from the sleeve. "I think that would probably be a big help to both Rosemary and Anna. You could help with the kids."

Emily wrinkled her nose. "But I'd want to be sewing, not—"

"Look who's here!" Aunt Rosemary's voice boomed as she slowly made her way back into the sewing room. "Bonnie stopped by for lace for Dana's veil."

Bonnie wore a pair of slacks and a rain jacket and held a bolt of white frilly stuff in her hands. "I heard your voices back here," she said.

Emily wanted to spread her body over the gowns, keeping them away from Bonnie Simons's gaze.

"Wow." Bonnie picked up a piece of interfacing from the pile for Michelle's dress. "It doesn't look like you've gotten anything done at all."

"Oh, that's not true." Aunt Rosemary tugged on each end of the tape measure around her neck. "All the hard part is done. It won't take us any time at all."

"Us?" Bonnie held the bolt of lace close to her bosom.

Aunt Rosemary grinned and then said, "I asked Emily if I could help—and she graciously accepted."

Emily ducked her head toward her machine so Bonnie wouldn't see her smile.

"Well, Dana has been a little worried about the dresses." Bonnie took a step closer to Emily.

"No worries." Grandma stood, the seam ripper still in her hand. "Everything is under control."

"Now, why don't I ring that up for you." Aunt Rosemary took the lace from Bonnie. "I know you probably have a million things to do today. Being the mother of the bride is a full-time job." The women walked back into the shop.

"I'm going to go too," Grandma said. "I'll be back at closing time to pick you up."

"Thanks," Emily said, standing. She gave Grandma a hug and said, "And thanks for standing up for me."

Grandma hugged her back. "Just get these dresses done, okay?"

Emily sat back down. It certainly wasn't going to be as easy as Aunt Rosemary had made it sound, but she felt better having her great-aunt in her corner. She sighed. And she owed Ashley an apology too.

THREE HOURS LATER Emily shivered as Grandma pulled into the driveway of Heather Creek Farm. "I think your heater is still broken," she said as the car came to a stop.

Grandma nodded. "I'd better have Grandpa take another look."

Emily yawned and then said, "I'm going to go say hi to the horses. Then I'll take my sewing stuff upstairs." She stepped onto the ground and stretched her back.

"I'll need help getting dinner on the table," Grandma said.

"I'll only be a minute." Emily pulled her hood onto her

head and began making her way across the muddy driveway. She turned toward the house at the sound of the back door slamming. Sam hurried across the lawn, Snowflake's bottle in his hand.

"How's your baby?" she asked Sam as he caught up with her, splattering mud on the legs of her jeans.

"Growing like a weed." Sam grinned.

"You might not think this is all fun and games when it's time to wean him." Emily knew she had that know-it-all tone to her voice. "Or when it comes time to haul him off to the butcher."

Sam just shrugged. He was such a goofball.

"What else did you do all day, besides play house?" she asked.

Sam shrugged. "Stuff. Computer games. Facebook. A little bit of homework."

"Homework? Really? Are you thinking about graduating after all?"

Sam nudged her. "Knock it off."

"'Cause I've heard it's a good idea. Even if you decide to go to community college."

Sam increased his step, leaving Emily behind.

"Hey." It was Uncle Pete, standing in the doorway to the shed. "Sam, have Emily feed the calf."

"Ahh," Sam called out as he reached the barn door.

"I'm serious."

"I was going to go see Britney," Emily said.

Uncle Pete ignored her and went back into the shed. Emily put her hand out for the bottle and went into the barn. Sam started to follow. "Go away," she hissed at him. "Scram. Or I'll tell Uncle Pete."

He looked dejected. "Make sure and give Snowflake a bottle of water afterward, okay? It's supposed to help keep him from getting sick again."

Emily ignored him. Snowflake started to bawl before she reached the pen. He stayed in the corner, dancing around a little. Finally Emily coaxed him out. She sat on a bale of hay, holding the bottle, feeling the tug of the calf. She closed her eyes, but all she could see was waves of royal blue fabric. "Oh, boy," she whispered. "I've got to finish those dresses before they drive me nuts."

Chapter Eleven

As Pastor Nathan read, "Love one another with brotherly affection. Outdo one another in showing honor," Charlotte caught movement out of the corner of her eye. She turned her head. It was Bonnie Simons stopping at the end of the last pew, her clipboard in one hand and a big old tape measure in the other. She wore a pleated royal blue skirt, nearly the same color as the bridesmaids' dresses, and a red jacket.

"Paul wrote those words to the Romans," Pastor Nathan said, "and also to us. We are a family. Families love each other and hold fast to what is good." He raised his hands. "Honor each other this week."

Bob nudged Charlotte and nodded toward Bonnie.

"I know," Charlotte whispered.

"What is she doing?" Bob asked, a little too loudly.

Charlotte shrugged and turned to greet Hannah and Frank, who stood behind them, and then made her way down the pew. By the time she reached the aisle, Bonnie was on the platform. Charlotte tensed. Couldn't she wait until the congregation had left the sanctuary?

Bonnie began to wave. Charlotte wondered if the woman was motioning to her or to someone behind her as she turned her head. No. Bonnie was trying to get Charlotte's attention. She started toward her.

"Where are Pete and Dana?" Bonnie asked.

"Probably down in the fellowship hall." Charlotte stopped at the edge of the platform.

"And how about Christopher? I wanted to talk to him about the candle lighting."

"Candle lighting? I thought he was going to be an usher."

"Dana wants candles too." Bonnie placed her clipboard and the industrial-sized tape measure on the pulpit. "And it's a five o'clock wedding so that should work fine."

"Has she asked him?"

Bonnie didn't seem to be listening. She picked up the tape measure and walked over to the floral display behind the pulpit. "I'm trying to get an idea of how big the arrangements with the candles should be so I can tell the florist. Dana wants—" She paused as she measured the arrangement one way and then the other. "—white tulips now. Not roses. And I plan to wire greenery around the candelabras." She turned back to Charlotte. "Do you mind gathering everyone together? Tell them to meet up here."

"Everyone?"

"Dana, Pete, Christopher. We can have a check-in session. I don't want to leave everything until the rehearsal. The sooner we address all these little details the better."

Charlotte tried to smile, but she was afraid it came across as more of a grimace. Bonnie didn't seem to notice. As Charlotte made her way up the aisle, she caught sight of Grandma Maxie sitting in the last pew. The older woman smiled and nodded gently. Charlotte waved and then moved on, taking a deep breath as she hurried down the stairs.

The after-church hustle and bustle of the fellowship hall always cheered Charlotte. She could sense the warmth of the community as she entered. The younger children ran in circles around their parents while the older children stood in little clumps here and there, talking among themselves. Christopher was at the cookie table, filling his hands. As she started toward him, she scanned the room for Pete and Dana. There they were, directly in front of her, chatting with Pastor Nathan.

"So Wednesday night then? After the prayer meeting?" Pastor said as he pushed his glasses higher on his nose.

Pete and Dana both agreed as Charlotte said hello to all three.

"We were just setting up a premarital counseling session," Pastor Nathan said, as he shook Charlotte's hand.

"Oh." Of course Pastor Nathan would want to meet with them.

"We've been amiss not to schedule something sooner," the pastor said. "But we still have time to cover all the basics."

Pete chuckled. "In just one session?"

"Oh no." Pastor Nathan patted Pete on the back. "Every Wednesday night until the wedding. That will give us three sessions."

"Oh." Pete took a step backward. "I see."

Charlotte smiled and said they needed to get back up to the sanctuary for a check-in session about the wedding plans.

"Do I need to come along?" Pastor Nathan asked.

"Oh, no," Charlotte quickly said. "Dana's mom just has a few questions—for us. That's all."

The pastor looked relieved as he said his good-byes and headed over to visit with Melody and Russ.

Charlotte motioned to Christopher as the three made their way toward the staircase. "Have you talked to Christopher about lighting the candles?" she asked Dana.

"Pardon?"

"You know. You want Christopher to light the candles, right?"

"Who said anything about candles?" Pete stopped on the staircase.

Dana shrugged. "Mom brought it up, but that was all. I haven't even talked to you about it." Dana scooted past Pete on the stairs and muttered, "Not that we've had that much time to talk."

"Maybe I misunderstood," Charlotte said. "You two go ahead. I'll wait for Christopher."

By the time Charlotte and Christopher reached the sanctuary, Bonnie had Pete holding one end of the tape measure while she held the other.

"Mom," Dana said, "ours isn't the first wedding that's ever been held here. I'm sure there's plenty of room."

"But it looks so tiny," Bonnie said.

"We have only three attendants each—it's actually a pretty small wedding."

Bonnie yanked the tape, and it sprung out of Pete's hand. She gave him an annoyed look and turned to Dana but then caught sight of Christopher. "There you are."

Christopher took a step closer to Charlotte.

"Let's talk about the candles now." As Bonnie clapped her hands together the pleats of her skirt swung back and forth.

Dana made a time-out sign, holding her hands up. "We haven't made a decision about candles. I haven't even talked to Pete about it yet, and besides, this is all stuff that we can discuss at the rehearsal."

"Oh, I don't think so," Bonnie said. "There will be plenty of other things to take care of then."

Christopher stepped behind Charlotte.

Dana scowled. Christopher moaned.

"Then it's settled." Bonnie handed the end of the tape back to Pete. "Come on up, Christopher. You don't have to practice right now—but I just want to prepare you for the task."

"Do I have to?" Christopher muttered to Charlotte.

"Sure," Charlotte said, wanting to add "if that's what Dana wants." She took a deep breath, remembering Pastor Nathan's closing comments. Then she tucked her head next to Christopher's. "This is our chance to love and honor Dana and her mother—to embrace our new family."

Christopher scowled.

Bonnie kept talking. "The florist has the lighter—it's a big old brass thing, very old-fashioned. You'll be able to practice using it at the rehearsal." She motioned for Christopher to come up onto the platform, waving her hand in a frantic gesture.

He stumbled up the steps, and she grabbed him by the shoulders and then shifted him around. "There will be an arrangement right over there." She had him pointed toward the far right corner of the platform. "And over there." She swung him around so he was facing the left corner of the platform, keeping her hands glued to his shoulders. "You're it as far as candlelighters. I hate it when there're two and they get out of sync and keep glancing over at each other to try to balance things out." Bonnie looked over her shoulder. "Don't you, Charlotte?"

Charlotte found herself nodding even though she thought the whole little dance of the candlelighters that went on at weddings was kind of cute, like a prelude to the antics of the flower girl and ring bearer.

Dana stood off to the side, her arms folded across her chest.

"So," Bonnie said to Christopher, "this is an important job. You'll set the tone of the entire wedding."

Christopher stood stiffly and silently.

"You'll walk up that aisle, up these steps, light the candles to the right and then the left. Then you'll walk back down, and the ceremony will begin. Of course, first you will have ushered the guests to their seats." Bonnie let go of his shoulders. "Got it?"

Christopher turned around slowly, his face ashen. "What about her honoring me?" he mouthed to Charlotte as he walked down the stairs.

Charlotte smiled at him, knowing it was a hard concept for him to understand.

Bonnie crossed her arms. "What else?" she asked Dana.

"There's nothing else," Dana said, dropping her arms to her side. "I think we're done."

Pete reached for Dana's hand, and he led her down the stairs. "Hey, this is going to be fun."

"Wait, you two." Bonnie took her tape measure back out of her box. "I need help with a few more things."

Pete's face fell and Dana frowned.

"I just want to map out where everyone is going to stand—to see how much room we have."

Dana turned toward her mother. "Mom, no. We'll do that at the rehearsal—when we can tell everyone where they're supposed to stand."

Bonnie raised her eyebrows. "Never mind," she said. "You go along. I'll do my thing here and see you back at the house."

Charlotte and Christopher followed Pete and Dana out of the church. No one said a word. *Love one another with brotherly affection*, Charlotte chanted silently. God had always used Bob and the children to teach her the hard things about his love, and now he was using another family to reinforce those lessons.

As Bob drove his truck down the highway toward the farm, Charlotte asked him to take another look at the heater in her car.

"The heater's fine," Bob said. "I checked it out, and there's nothing wrong with it."

"Well, something's wrong with the car. It was cold the whole way into town yesterday."

"It probably didn't have time to warm up properly," Bob said.

Charlotte shook her head.

"Uncle Pete thought it was the thermostat," Sam said from the backseat.

"No, I checked that." Bob paused and then muttered, "At least I think I did."

Charlotte stared straight ahead, determined not to respond to Bob. He'd take care of the problem eventually.

She was tired. A nap after lunch sounded good, and then

she would finish the bureau runner she was embroidering for Dana's shower next week. It had a spray of posies in the middle and on each end. Hannah, Melody, and Rosemary were hosting the shower. She yawned, wondering if Rosemary had made an apron for Dana; she often did that for a bridal shower.

There was nothing like the group of women at Bedford Community Church to do things right by a bride.

"I'll take a look at your car again tomorrow," Bob said, stifling a yawn. "Today, I'm going to rest."

Chapter Twelve

Emily settled into her place in art class beside Ashley. Her friend gave her a stilted smile and then directed her attention to the front of the room.

Miss Carey stood in front of the art class, holding a Georgia O'Keeffe print of an oversize poppy. "With all the snow and now the rain, I thought we could use a little color around here," she said. "This next unit is going to explore the style of Georgia O'Keeffe. We're going to explore contour drawing, cropping, and layering of colors to show value changes."

She moved over to the display table. "I splurged and bought some flowers yesterday when I was in Harding." She motioned to the red roses and pink lilies in a vase. "And I borrowed these bones from the science department." There was a calf skull—which made Emily think of Snowflake—and some bones. "Georgia O'Keeffe is famous for her close-up flowers and for the bones and skull paintings she did after she moved to New Mexico."

Miss Carey placed the print on an easel behind her. More prints were taped along the top. "You can get some ideas from her work. The idea is to crop the object in a new way and show what you see."

Students started milling around, collecting newsprint and paints, pencils and paintbrushes. Emily pulled a pink lily from the vase, gathered supplies, and headed back to her table.

"How are the dresses coming along?" Ashley asked as she drew the calf skull on her paper. It seemed a little goth for Ashley.

"Okay. Aunt Rosemary is going to help me." Emily felt that little tug inside.

"Oh really. Why?" Ashley's voice sounded a little weird.

"'Cause they're hard." Emily erased a line from her flower and then tried again. She knew she needed to tell Ashley that she'd messed up cutting her dress out too.

"Your skull looks cool," she said to Ashley.

"Thanks. Mind if I look over at your lily? I could use some color."

Emily moved the lily between them as Miss Carey stopped in front of Emily and Ashley's table. "Emily, I heard that you're making the bridesmaids' dresses for Dana's—I mean Miss Simons's—wedding."

Emily nodded, stealing a look at Ashley.

"That's a big job. Not many experienced seamstresses—unless they're professional—would take that on."

Miss Carey drummed her fingers on the tabletop. "And Miss Simons said that you were willing to make her dress too."

"That was before I said I'd do the bridesmaids' dresses," Emily explained. "I couldn't have sewn all of them."

Ashley looked up from her drawing. "Miss Simons is wearing my mother's dress." Emily expected her to say that it was a designer gown that originally came from New York, but she didn't.

Miss Carey tilted her head. "Are your mom and Miss Simons friends?"

"They went to school together," Ashley explained.

Emily wanted to say that her mother had gone to school with them too, but she didn't want Miss Carey to ask any more questions so she said, "That's how Miss Simons knows my Uncle Pete. They were high school sweethearts."

Miss Carey smiled. "I didn't realize that. Wow. Only in a small town." She commented on Ashley's skull and then walked around the table to calm down the rowdy boys in the back.

"I think my mom was hoping I'd wear her dress someday," Ashley said, "but I told her no way. It's definitely out of style."

Emily tried to smile, but instead her eye twitched. She'd give anything to have her mother's dress to wear, give anything for her mom to have had a big church wedding in Bedford instead of getting married by a justice of the peace in San Diego, all alone with no family beside her. Emily shivered a little, her thoughts turning back to Melody and the cancer that she had beaten, and a feeling of gratitude replaced Emily's grief.

"I'm not working after school. Do you want to come over and hang out?" Ashley asked.

Picking up her pencil, Emily shook her head. "I'm going over to Fabrics and Fun. Anna is going to be there with her kids—to get help sewing Madison's and Jennifer's flower girl dresses."

"That sounds like fun." Ashley stood and eyed the lily.

"Ashley." Emily's voice shook a little. "I need to apologize to you for getting upset about your cutting the sleeve out wrong. I'm sorry."

"Thanks." Ashley's voice was quiet and matter of fact.

Emily smiled. There. She'd apologized. But for some reason she couldn't quite admit that she had cut the sleeves for her dress out wrong too.

EMILY COULDN'T FIND SAM after school. He wasn't at his locker or hanging out with his buddies, who were flipping their skateboards off the front steps. By the time she reached the parking lot his car was gone. She stood with her hands on her hips.

"He gave Arielle a ride," Ashley called out from the other side of the parking lot. "They just left."

"He has my sewing machine in the back of his car." She fished her cell out of her pocket and dialed Sam. He didn't answer.

"Want to walk with me?"

Emily nodded. She might as well go on to Fabrics and Fun. Maybe Sam would check his phone or come to his senses and stop by.

As they walked, it started to rain. At first it was just a drizzle, but soon it turned into a steady drip as the girls passed the town library and then crossed Farnham Street. The school bus lumbered by, and Emily searched the windows.

There was Christopher, toward the back of the bus, waving, the start of a smile on his face. Emily waved back and then swiped her damp bangs across her forehead. Her jacket didn't have a hood. That Sam. Always thinking about himself instead of others.

Ashley pulled an umbrella from her book bag and popped it open, positioning it so it covered Emily too.

"Do you know, has Miss Simons had your mom's dress altered?"

"Quite a while ago," Ashley said.

"Who did it?" Emily asked.

"Your Aunt Rosemary." Ashley quickened her step.

Emily hurried her pace to keep up with Ashley. Aunt Rosemary sure was doing a lot for Miss Simons and Uncle Pete's wedding.

"Have you been riding your horses lately?" Ashley asked as they walked along Morley Park.

Emily shook her head. "I haven't had time." She quickened her step again. Sam's car was parked in front of Jenny's Creamery. "Thanks, Ashley," she said. "I need to catch Sam."

She started to run as Sam headed across the street from the pharmacy. "Sam," she called out. He was running—his sweatshirt unzipped, his hood off—and he quickly reached his car, flinging open the door.

"Sam!" she yelled again, racing down the sidewalk. Just as he started to pull his car away, Emily slapped the back of it. He stopped. She slapped it again.

"Hey." He stepped out of the car. "Emily, what are you doing?"

She bent over, her hands on her knees, panting. "My

machine. You were supposed to give me a ride to Fabrics and Fun."

"Oh." He opened the back of his car and motioned with his hand.

"Can you get it?"

"No. I need to get home."

She yanked the machine out. "Do you ever think about actually helping? About other people's needs instead of just your own?"

"I'm not thinking about myself any more than you are."

"What? I'm making these dresses for Uncle Pete and Miss Simons's wedding, in case you haven't noticed."

Sam crossed his arms. "You're making those dresses to draw attention to yourself, out of your own stupid pride."

Emily's face grew hot even in the cold air, even with rain dripping down it. "What?"

"Emily, need some help?" Ashley stood behind her, the umbrella still over her head.

"Here," Emily said, shoving the bag of fabric at her. "Take this."

Sam slammed the hatchback down. "Have fun," he said. He smirked, climbed back into his car, and revved the motor.

WHILE EMILY SET UP her sewing machine in the back room, Madison and Jennifer hovered around her, chattering away about their dresses. Jennifer's hair was pulled back in a ponytail that looked like she had done it herself, and Madison's hair swung long and straight, instead of in her usual perfect braids.

Ashley stood beside Aunt Anna and stroked Will's arm. "He's so cute," Ashley said. "How old is he?"

Emily couldn't help but watch her friend playing with her youngest cousin. Will was nearly bald, and drool cascaded over his lower lip, but he was cute. Not quite as cute as Christopher had been with his full head of fine blond hair and big eyes, but still, he was a sweet-looking baby.

"He'll be four months in another week." Aunt Anna swayed back and forth.

The baby turned his face toward Ashley and smiled.

"May I hold him?" Ashley asked.

Aunt Anna hesitated and Emily turned her head, pretending not to be observing. "After you wash your hands," her aunt finally said. As Ashley headed for the restroom, Aunt Anna turned toward Emily. "How long can you stay today?"

"Until Grandma comes—probably around five thirty."

"Oh, good. I'm going to need a lot of help. I've only just started the girls' dresses." She picked up a piece of white fabric with her free hand. "Rosemary said she would help. But I haven't done a thing on my skirt."

"Your skirt?"

Aunt Anna laid the white fabric on the table and pulled royal blue fabric from a basket. "I found this in Harding a couple of weeks ago. Isn't it gorgeous?"

Emily could feel her eyes grow wide. It was the fabric for the bridesmaids' dresses. "Um, Aunt Anna," she said, lifting her dress from the bag Ashley had carried in. "I think your fabric is the same as—" She flung out her dress. "—mine. And the other bridesmaids'."

"Oh, what a coincidence," Aunt Anna said, standing tall, looking Emily in the eye.

Emily couldn't hold her gaze. If only Grandma or Aunt Rosemary were in the room. She pulled the beginning of Michelle's dress out of the bag, trying to look busy as Ashley came back into the room and took Will from Aunt Anna.

Aunt Anna sat down at her machine. "Well, I certainly don't want to look like one of the bridesmaids."

"Can't you just buy a dress?" Emily said, her voice shaky. "It would save you time. Or wear one of those pretty dresses you already have?"

Aunt Anna inhaled and then exhaled slowly. "The pattern I picked out is perfect."

Emily shook her head. "Aunt Anna, don't you think it will look odd if you use the same material?"

Her aunt's lips moved into an ice-queen smile.

"I can stay and help with the kids," Ashley said.

Aunt Anna turned her attention to Ashley. "Maybe for a little while. Then Emily can take a turn with Will." Ashley headed toward the far end of the room, the baby in her arms and Madison and Jennifer tagging along.

"Well, well," Aunt Rosemary boomed, coming into the sewing room. "I hate to wish customers away, but we'd better make some progress here." She stopped in her tracks and looked from Emily to Aunt Anna. "What's going on in here? The start of World War III?"

Emily sighed.

Aunt Anna excused herself to the restroom.

Emily pointed to her dress and then to Anna's fabric.

Aunt Rosemary sank into a chair, chuckling, and said, "So Anna stabbed me in the back too?"

"Looks that way," Emily said. "And she's looking to stab me now. She really likes this fabric."

Aunt Rosemary sighed. "Just see how it plays out, Emily. Don't get into a power play over it though, okay?"

Emily shrugged. She couldn't comprehend how Aunt Anna thought her skirt was as important as the bridesmaids' dresses.

AUNT ROSEMARY PUT the zipper in Emily's dress, which left only the hem and the trim to do. The cascading flounce and the pleated trim intimidated her almost as much as the sleeves, but she didn't want to ask Aunt Rosemary for help now because she was finishing Jennifer's dress.

Ashley handed the baby to Emily. "I need to get going." It was almost five. "I think he needs his diaper changed," she said. "Sorry."

Aunt Anna thanked Ashley as she left and resumed her sewing on Madison's dress.

Will began to fuss as Emily dug through his bag. Madison pulled out the diaper-changing pad and spread it across the back table, and Emily lowered the baby onto it. Now he was howling.

"Oh, for goodness' sake," Aunt Anna said, standing.

Emily wrestled the baby down and was taking off his diaper when her aunt said, "I'll do it."

"Mama, can we go home?" Jennifer asked.

"In a little bit." Aunt Anna quickly changed the diaper and handed Will back to Emily while she went to the restroom to wash her hands.

"I'm hungry," Jennifer said. Madison pulled some fish

crackers from the diaper bag, and the girls sat side by side on the same chair. Whenever Emily was with them, she wished she had a sister. She began walking Will around the room.

Aunt Anna returned and reached out her arms for the baby. "He's hungry," she said and settled down into a chair with him. "Emily, do you mind completing the seam on Madison's dress? It's halfway done—just finish it on my machine." Aunt Anna looked at the baby while she fed him. "I sure wish Charlotte had been able to come help today," she said.

Emily wasn't sure why Grandma hadn't come to help or if she'd even been asked. She sat down at Aunt Anna's machine and finished the seam, but when she turned the fabric over to cut the thread she realized the tension in the bobbin had been off and there was a mess on the backside. She reached for the seam ripper and began pulling it out. She worked carefully, trying not to puncture the fabric.

Her eyes darted over to her own machine. Michelle expected to be fitted in a week. And Emily still needed to make Amber's dress and the three shawls. They needed a fringe that would match the pleated trim on the dresses. That would take extra time too.

Aunt Anna stood over Emily with Will a few minutes later. "Do you mind holding him while I pack up?" When Emily stood and Aunt Anna saw the messy seam she rolled her eyes. "I thought you could sew."

"I can," Emily answered. "There was something wrong with your machine."

"It worked fine for me." Aunt Anna sat down.

Emily shuffled around with the baby, bouncing him every time he started to fuss. The girls played with little dolls on the far table. Anxiety welled in Emily, and she hoped Aunt Anna didn't plan to sew with Aunt Rosemary tomorrow. It was too stressful.

"Hello!"

Emily turned toward the shop door, relieved to hear Grandma's voice. Madison and Jennifer squealed, jumped down from their chairs, and ran toward Grandma, mobbing her as she came through the doorway. Emily followed them, offering up the baby. Grandma hugged the little girls and then took Will in her arms. He smiled.

Emily jetted back to her sewing machine and Michelle's dress. If she could sew after school every day this week, she would finish Michelle's dress on time. Maybe, if Aunt Anna didn't come around, Aunt Rosemary would do the other two zippers for her too.

"Aunt Anna," Emily said, "doesn't your mother sew?"

Aunt Anna sighed again. "She used to, but her arthritis is so bad in her hands that it's really painful for her. In fact, it's getting too hard for her to even change Will's diaper."

"Oh, dear," Aunt Rosemary said, standing. "That's a pity." Aunt Rosemary held out her hands and moved her fingers up and down. Then she steadied herself against the table. "My hands are fine," she said, "but my balance isn't as good as it used to be."

Emily glanced around. Grandma was looking at Jennifer's and Madison's dolls and hadn't heard Aunt Rosemary. Aunt Anna didn't seem worried.

Later, on the way home, Emily told Grandma about

Aunt Anna purchasing the same material. "It's so obviously bridesmaid-dress material."

"It's nice fabric," Grandma said. "Take it as a compliment that Anna picked it out too."

"But it's too bright for her."

"She wears colors nicely."

Emily crossed her arms. "But the bridesmaids' dresses are what's most important," she wailed. "It's ridiculous that she's not cooperating."

"Give it time," Grandma said. "And don't be dramatic about it, Emily, please. The last thing we need right now is more drama. Planning a wedding right now is plenty."

Emily sank back against the seat. "What do you mean?"

"Don't make a big deal about the duplicate fabric. Don't talk it up to everyone."

"Like?"

"To Dana and Pete. To Sam. To Ashley. You know, just concentrate on making the dresses—not on gossiping."

Emily's face grew warm, even though the car was freezing. "When are you going to get the heater fixed?"

"Grandpa ordered a new part," Grandma said, her voice still firm.

Emily turned toward the window and pressed her nose against the cold glass. When she got married—it would be when she was twenty-nine—she was going to buy a designer gown, maybe Vera Wang. And she'd only have one bridesmaid, probably Ashley. And she wasn't going to invite Aunt Anna—but she would want Madison, Jennifer, and Will to come. Being part of a family sure was awkward.

Chapter Thirteen

Toby ran ahead of Charlotte as she headed to the mailbox, chasing a crow that hopped along the ground. The bird took off, swooping up to a poplar tree in the windbreak. The crow cawed as Toby circled around the base of the tree before giving up and heading back to the road.

The bus appeared over the rise in the road as Charlotte closed the mailbox, clutching the stack of envelopes in her hand. Christopher bounced down the steps of the bus and bent down to pet Toby. Next came Emily, looking forlorn.

"Why aren't you at Fabrics and Fun?" Charlotte asked.

"Aunt Rosemary called the school and told me not to come. She's not feeling well." Emily swung her book bag over her shoulder as she walked beside Charlotte. "She told me to come tomorrow."

"Oh, dear. Do you want me to take you into town to get your stuff?" Emily had left her machine and material at Rosemary's yesterday since she planned to go again after school today. Charlotte had hoped a third sewing day in a row would really move things along.

Emily shook her head. "She closed the shop for the afternoon. Besides, I need a day off from all of that. I think I'll take Britney out for a ride."

Charlotte cast a look toward the horizon. The sky was clear except for a few white, fluffy clouds. Pete had been plowing all day again. He'd come by the house for a sandwich but that was all.

"Do you want to ride with me, Grandma?" Emily asked.

Charlotte hesitated. It had been a long time since Emily last invited her to ride, but she still had dinner to fix and laundry to finish. "Just a short ride, okay?"

Emily insisted she didn't need a snack and quickly gathered a couple of sweatshirts from upstairs. Christopher started on his homework while Charlotte quickly folded a load of laundry.

"Come on," Emily said, standing by the back door.

Charlotte grabbed her brown coat and followed her granddaughter out to the barn.

"You'd be proud of me," Emily said. "I didn't tell anyone about Aunt Anna and the fabric fiasco. I didn't bring it up with Ashley—and she already knows about it."

"And Ashley didn't bring it up?" Charlotte asked.

"Nope."

As they neared the barn, they could hear Snowflake crying in the corral. The graft cow was mooing, and her swollen udder made it obvious that Snowflake hadn't nursed her. Charlotte had thought the calf would graft, but it was getting pretty obvious that Snowflake was going to be a bottle-fed calf. At fifty-five dollars a jar, the calf formula was really starting to add up.

"Come on," Emily said, pushing the barn door open.

Charlotte adjusted her eyes and followed Emily to Britney's stall. The horse nodded her head up and down and stepped toward the railing. Emily got her a bucket of oats, and Charlotte grabbed the comb and started in on her tail.

"It's pretty tangled, huh?" Emily said.

"A little." Charlotte kept at it. It was obvious that the horses had been neglected lately.

"Do you think I can start breaking Stormy this summer?" Emily began brushing the horse's flank as she talked.

"Ask your uncle."

Pete would have to help. Breaking a colt took a lot of knowledge and stamina.

"I've missed the horses," Emily said.

"They take a lot of time." Charlotte pulled the hair from the comb.

"I know. It's hard to make time for sewing *and* riding."

"You can't do everything," Charlotte said. "Some things have to take a backseat."

Emily nodded, but the frown still hung on her face. "It's enough just trying to keep up with my homework."

Alarmed, Charlotte said, "Are you behind?" She rarely even checked with Emily about her schoolwork because she was always on top of it.

"No." Emily paused. "Well, I have questions to do for history tonight—but I'll get it done."

Charlotte continued working on Britney's mane. She was hoping the ride would be good for Emily, even though usually she would insist her granddaughter finish her homework first. Emily seemed so stressed lately though, and she couldn't ride after dark. The exercise and fresh air would do her good.

A few minutes later, Charlotte put the halter on Britney while Emily swung on the saddle and then cinched it. "We should get going," Charlotte said. She had a roast and vegetables in the slow cooker, but she still needed to make a salad.

Together, they groomed and saddled Shania and then led the horses out the barn door.

As they rode along the creek, Emily led the way and Charlotte followed breathing in the crisp spring air. The trail was muddy and slick, and she slowed Shania, but Emily trotted ahead under the budding weeping willow trees. There were worse things than Emily being too busy, and it was just for a season. Charlotte thought about when Denise was a cheerleader and struggled to keep up with the horses too. Through the years Bob had lobbied to get rid of the horses—hay burners, he called them—but Charlotte and Pete had both convinced him not to.

For years she had felt that Denise might come back to Bedford; if her family didn't draw her home, maybe her horses would. It had been a silly thing to hold on to, but now with Emily on the farm she was thankful she hadn't given in to Bob. The horses were both a connection that she had with Emily and one that Emily had with her mother.

The path turned away from the creek, and Charlotte urged Shania up the slope. Emily stopped Britney at the top of the incline. She smiled as Charlotte approached.

"Thanks for riding with me, Grandma. I feel so much better."

Charlotte nodded. Crisp air. The rhythm of a horse. Time to think. It worked every time.

AS CHARLOTTE WALKED BACK to the house, Sam swung his car into the driveway and then opened his window. "Am I too late to feed Snowflake?" he called out.

Charlotte shook her head. "He's been in the corral all day. With the cow." She waited for Sam as he parked his car.

"Can I get him out?"

Charlotte turned toward the Home Quarter. She could make out the tractor, just a little spot in the distance. Pete wouldn't be home anytime soon. She might as well make the decision. "Okay."

When she got back into the house, Christopher was just hanging up the phone. "Miss Simons called for Uncle Pete—she wants him to call her back ASAP."

"Any other phone calls?" Charlotte asked, rubbing her hands together.

"Yeah, someone else called for Uncle Pete. They just left a number." Christopher held up the message pad on the table. "I wrote it down—right here."

AFTER DINNER AND THE DISHES, as Charlotte wiped the counters down, Emily sat down at the dining room table. "Boy, Uncle Pete sure is working late," she said, opening her notebook.

"Well that's the life of a farmer," Charlotte answered. "You have to do what you can when you can. You know, headlights on tractors way back in the 1930s changed everything . . ."

Emily interrupted. "Isn't he supposed to meet with the pastor tonight?"

Charlotte froze. Tonight was Wednesday.

"With Miss Simons? For their pre . . . pre-mar-i-tal coun-se-ling." Emily pronounced each syllable. "Whatever that is."

"Oh, dear," Charlotte said. It was seven fifteen. Pastor Nathan expected them by eight.

"Bob," Charlotte called, stepping toward the family room. "Can you—" He was asleep in his chair. If she woke him up he would be grumpy and complain about Pete being irresponsible.

Charlotte started up the stairs. "Sam!" She would send him down to the Home Quarter to get Pete's attention.

Chapter Fourteen

Pete shifted the tractor all the way down and then turned the motor off. He jumped down to the ground and then reached up and slammed the door shut behind him. He was done with the Home Quarter. It was completely plowed and ready for the corn to be seeded. He would move the tractor in the morning and plow some more and hopefully start the seeding next week.

He lifted his arms over his head, stretching his back. Sitting like that was hard work. That padded seat with the adjustable lumbar cushion on the new John Deere model sure would make life easier.

As he climbed into his pickup, car lights drifted toward him. It was probably Dad, checking up on him.

He started his truck and pulled onto the dirt road. The oncoming vehicle was a car, not a pickup.

He rolled down his window as the car grew closer. It was Sam, veering too far toward the ditch as he approached Pete.

"Hey," Pete called out. He didn't want to have to pull Sam out of the ditch. "Watch it," he said as Sam rolled down his window.

"Grandma said for you to hurry or you'll be late for your meeting."

"Meeting?" His volunteer firefighter meeting had been last night.

"At the church." Sam gripped the steering wheel.

"The church." Pete felt like an idiot. He vaguely remembered a meeting at the church. "Is today Wednesday?"

Sam nodded. "You okay, Uncle Pete?"

Pete shook his head. "No, I'm not okay. I'm headed to the doghouse, for good this time."

Sam backed up and then turned around, struggling in the mud. Pete held his breath, terrified his nephew was going to get stuck, but Sam gunned it and pushed ahead. Pete followed.

It was five past eight by the time he left the house, his hair still dripping wet. He'd hardly dried off; his shirt stuck to his back.

Maybe Dana was right to be exasperated with him. Maybe Dad was right too. The meeting with the pastor was the most important thing he had going all week, besides the plowing and the seeding and everything else. Dana would never understand. Hopefully she wouldn't tell her mother.

He pulled out onto the highway and accelerated, speeding past Hannah and Frank's house. The stars were bright in the cold sky, and the darkness seemed endless before him. Driving into town seemed to be taking forever. He glanced at the clock on his dashboard—8:10, give or take a couple of minutes. He should have asked Mom to call the church, but then Dana would feel like he was relying on Mom to rescue him.

As he turned onto Main Street, he hoped that Dana had gone home. He could make up some excuse—say his truck broke down. He shook his head. Nah. He wouldn't lie to Dana, no matter how badly he wanted to cover his sorry behind. He pulled into the parking lot and flung open the door, leaping to the pavement.

"Pete Stevenson." Bonnie Simons stood at the entrance to the church, her clipboard in her hand. "What do you have to say for yourself?"

Pete flinched as if he'd been hit. "Whoa. What are you doing here?"

"Checking out the floral pillars." Bonnie zipped her coat, the clipboard tucked under her arm. "Why are you late?"

Pete waved as he walked by her. "I've got a beautiful lady waiting for me—I've got to go." He hurried down the hall toward the pastor's office. He hadn't felt like such a heel in a long time.

"SO," PASTOR NATHAN said an hour later, standing up from his chair. "I think we're off to a good start. I'll see you next week—same place."

Pete stood too and shoved his hands into his jeans pockets.

"But on time." Pastor Nathan chuckled. "You know . . ." He'd grown suddenly serious. ". . . you wouldn't start a business venture without learning what you needed to know to make it work. It's the same with marriage."

Dana gathered her coat and purse.

"And," Pastor Nathan continued, "as you know, half of

all marriages end in divorce and half of the marriages that make it aren't happy ones."

Dana let out what could have been a chuckle—or maybe a gasp—and Pete sat back down in his chair, feeling like he'd just been kicked in the gut.

Pastor Nathan chuckled again. "So do you see why premarital counseling is important?" He extended his hand to Pete and pulled him from the chair. Pete stepped back and let Dana walk out of the office first.

"Did you drive?" Pete asked as they walked into the narthex.

"No. Mom gave me a ride, but I'm sure she's already gone. Can you give me a ride home?"

Pete hurried around to the passenger side of his pickup.

"I phoned out to the farm and talked to Christopher earlier," Dana said, climbing into the pickup. "To tell you what the plan was."

"He didn't say anything." Pete slammed the door and resumed the conversation once he climbed up onto the bench seat. "I was out plowing all day again."

"And evening?" Dana asked.

"Yep."

They drove along in silence for a minute.

"That was a pretty grim statistic that Pastor Nathan quoted." Dana clung to her purse.

Pete nodded. "Hope he doesn't bring that up at the wedding."

Dana paused and then said, "Me too."

Pete glanced her way. She wasn't smiling.

"What are you thinking about?" Pete asked.

"Happy marriages. Do you think your parents are happy?" she asked.

"Happy enough." Pete had actually never wondered about his parents' marriage. They seemed content though. "What about yours?"

"Oh, you know," she said. "Dad seems happy, but I think Mom's childhood keeps her from being as happy as she could be. She's had a hard life. Her mother died when she was little, and her dad passed away right before she married." Dana sighed. "I guess Mom is happy, but Dad and I are all she has. And Grandma Maxie, but it's not quite the same. And Mom has always been uptight—a perfectionist, you know?"

Pete did know.

"But . . ." Dana continued talking, and Pete concentrated on listening. ". . . Grandma Maxie and Grandpa Simons had a good relationship. Even when they were old, they still held hands and kissed." She smiled. "I remember that clearly. They adored each other." She sighed.

Pete felt like he was supposed to say something; he just wasn't sure what.

THE NEXT MORNING, he was surprised to find Snowflake back in the barn; he turned on his heels, storming back into the house.

"Who put the calf back in his pen?" he called out as he clamored through the back door.

"I told Sam to," his mom answered from the laundry room. "He didn't take to the cow in the corral, not at all. They were both miserable."

Pete slung the pail onto the counter. "Well, that's it I guess. I've failed."

Mom stepped into the kitchen, a stack of towels in her arms. "You haven't failed. Sometimes a calf just won't graft. That's all."

"Dad's going to be ticked."

"Pete." She looked over her shoulder as she headed back down the hall. "Stop fretting about the calf."

He poured himself a cup of coffee and sat down at the table. It was another clear day, and the mud had dried a little more. A pad of paper was on the table too. It read "Pete" at the top and then a number was written down. Then farther down on the page were the words, "Dana called." It looked like Christopher's handwriting. That must have been the message he missed yesterday.

Mom came back into the kitchen.

"Do you know what this message is about?" Pete asked, pointing at the first one.

She shook her head. "Christopher took it, but he said the man didn't leave any details."

Pete read the number again. He didn't recognize it.

"How was the counseling session?" she asked.

"Depressing." Pete took a long sip of hot coffee, hoping the caffeine would kick in soon.

"Why?"

"It turns out that I'm joining the ranks of a multitude of unhappy people." He took another drink of scalding coffee.

"Who says?"

"Pastor Nathan." Pete stood.

"Well." As Mom spoke, his dad shuffled into the room. "People are usually as happy as they want to be."

Pete shook his head as he grabbed the phone from the wall and dialed the number. Of course he wanted to be happy. He just wasn't sure he could make Dana happy. The phone rang and rang, but no one picked up and an answering machine didn't click on. "Christopher didn't have a clue who called?" he asked as he hung up the phone.

"I don't think so," Mom said.

"Couldn't have been that important," Pete said, placing his coffee cup in the sink. "I'm off to the field."

"What about breakfast?" Mom asked.

"No, thanks."

Dad asked. "What's for breakfast?"

Pete waved his hand and slipped through the back door, not wanting to stick around for any questions about the calf, the plowing, the seeding, the unattainable tractor, or anything else that had to do with the farm.

Chapter Fifteen

Charlotte grabbed Christopher's paper lunch sack off the table and hurried out the back door, still wearing her slippers, waving her arms and hoping Sam would see her in the rearview mirror of his car.

The 240-Z accelerated around the curve in the driveway and then slowed. Emily rolled down her window as the car began traveling in reverse. Charlotte jogged to meet it.

"Thanks." Christopher stuck his head out the window, craning his neck from the backseat.

As Charlotte waved to the kids, she felt dampness seeping through the bottom of her slippers. She turned and walked along the high center ridge in the driveway.

"Char." Bob stood in the doorway to the shed, a greasy rag over his shoulder and a wrench in his hand. "I put in that new thermostat. I got it at the surplus place in Harding for quite a deal. Want to take the car for a spin?"

So Pete had been right—not that Bob was admitting so. She looked down at her slippers. "I'll be back out in a minute." She hurried into the house and picked up the phone, giving Hannah a quick call to see if she had time for a cup of coffee.

"I just started the second pot of the morning," Hannah said. "Come on down."

A few minutes later Bob backed Charlotte's Ford Focus out of the shed. "That hardly cost a thing," Bob said as he climbed out of the driver's seat.

Charlotte took Bob's hand and squeezed it. "Thank you," she said. "What are you going to do to keep busy for the rest of the morning?"

Bob folded the rag and placed it on his workbench. "I think I'll read the paper."

"Do you want to ride down to Hannah's with me?"

He looked as if he were considering it for a moment and then said, "Better not. Frank is probably out plowing—I'd just be a third wheel."

Charlotte kissed his cheek, thanked him again, and climbed into her car. He wouldn't enjoy having coffee with her and Hannah.

A few minutes later she pulled into her friend's driveway, put the car into park, and made her way through the mud to the back door. Hannah was in the doorway before Charlotte had a chance to knock, giving her a hug and urging her to take off her boots and coat. The kitchen smelled delicious.

"I've been testing recipes," Hannah explained. "You're just in time to give me your opinion."

Charlotte looked down at the countertop. There was a platter of cupcakes and what looked like a cheesecake. "Are these for the shower?" Charlotte asked.

Hannah nodded, picking up a knife. "You're my taste tester. Raspberry cheesecake and hazelnut truffle cupcakes."

"You don't have to twist my arm," Charlotte said, opening the cupboard door and taking down two of Hannah's white dessert plates. The shower was going to be next Tuesday evening, the only evening that would work for Dana's cousin Michelle—who had just started working as a nurse in Harding—and the church schedule. "It's awfully nice of you to help with the shower." Charlotte set the plates by the desserts.

"Well, I wouldn't have it any other way." Hannah sliced the cheesecake. "You know, there were years when I didn't think that Pete would ever get married, but I kept praying that God would bring the right young woman into his life."

Charlotte had no idea that Hannah had been praying for a wife for Pete. She sighed. Honestly, there had been years when she had stopped praying for Pete's wife, convinced he'd remain a bachelor.

"Pete has turned into a nice young man," Hannah added.

Charlotte smiled. He wasn't so young anymore, actually, but it was sweet that Hannah thought of him that way.

Hannah lifted a piece of the cheesecake onto a plate as Charlotte poured a little milk into two cups. "Melody is coming up with the entertainment."

Charlotte chuckled as she poured the coffee. "That should be fun. Are we going to square dance? Maybe hula hoop?"

Hannah iced one of the hazelnut truffle cupcakes. "I can't tell or you might feel like you have to prepare for it." She grinned again, pushing back a strand of blonde hair that had fallen across her face. "But it's going to be a lot of fun."

The church showers always were enjoyable, and the women were so generous, turning out in droves, even if they didn't know the bride very well.

"We were wondering if Emily could help at the shower." Hannah placed both plates on the table. "If she can clear plates—that sort of thing."

"I'm sure she would." Charlotte put the coffee on the

table and sat down. Hopefully Emily would get a lot of sewing done before then.

"We'll have you and Emily and Bonnie all sit in the front—and Dana's cousin too. Michelle? Isn't that her name?"

Charlotte nodded.

"It's been good to see Bonnie around town again. In fact, I saw her Wednesday night after Bible study. I'm not sure why she was there, though, because she didn't join us."

Charlotte held her fork, loaded with cheesecake, in midair. "She was at the church? On Wednesday?"

Hannah nodded.

Charlotte cringed as she took the bite of cheesecake, wondering if Bonnie had been there for the counseling session. No wonder Pete was in a funk. "Delicious," Charlotte declared after she'd swallowed.

"How's the wedding planning coming?" Hannah asked.

"It's been pretty painless for me." Charlotte stirred her coffee. "I know things will get busy closer to the wedding, but so far so good." She took a bite of the truffle cupcake. It was delicious too. "So I have to choose between the two?" she asked her friend.

Hannah held up her cupcake. "Maybe not." She smiled. "How about if I make both?"

Thrilled that Hannah had come to the conclusion on her own, Charlotte agreed.

"SO THE CAR WAS OKAY?" Bob asked in the afternoon as Charlotte settled into her chair to rest for a few minutes before Christopher came home from school.

"Char?"

"Bob, I've told you at least three times already that it worked fine. I'll let you know when I get back from town with Emily though, okay?"

He pulled his reading glasses from his pocket and unfolded the *Bedford Leader* with a snap.

"I'm sorry." She hadn't meant to be testy. The car had kept him busy for the last couple of days, but now he needed something more to do.

Charlotte closed her eyes. The more proficient Pete got with the farm, the less he needed Bob's help. Hannah was right; Pete had turned out just fine. He had just been a late bloomer. She wished she could have known when he dropped out of high school and was in his difficult stage that all of that wouldn't matter in another fourteen years. She sighed a little, which Bob must have taken as an invitation to talk to her.

She could hear him folding the newspaper, and then he said, "I'm so pleased with how inexpensive it was to fix your car."

Charlotte kept her eyes closed as she nodded. Maybe he would get the hint that she wanted to rest a little.

"Char?"

She opened her eyes. "Have you thought about a hobby you could take up?" she asked, turning her head toward him slightly.

He peered at her over his reading glasses. "I was thinking that maybe I could open a repair shop."

Charlotte's stomach sank as she imagined the driveway filled with spare parts and broken-down vehicles. "Hmm," she said, closing her eyes. If there was one thing she had learned from being a mother, grandmother, and wife, it was to not overreact. Bob was probably just thinking out loud. The best thing to do was ignore him.

CHARLOTTE STOOD at the kitchen window. Christopher was running toward the house from the barn, yelling something, with Toby jumping along beside him. He didn't seem to be hurt. She hurried to the back door.

"Grandma!"

She opened the door. "What is it, sweetie?"

"I want to show you something."

"Is everything all right?" As she spoke, she looked at her grandson standing in the open doorway, letting in the chilly air.

"It's a surprise." His eyes twinkled.

Charlotte relaxed. She'd been afraid that something had happened to the calf. She stumbled over her muddy slippers—she'd meant to wash them after she got back from Hannah's—to put on her boots. Emily had gone to Rosemary's again to sew, and Sam had stayed in town after school.

Charlotte followed Christopher across the lawn.

"It's on the far side of the barn, on the outside." Christopher picked up a stick and lobbed it across the driveway and Toby scampered ahead. Christopher broke into a jog and then turned the corner of the barn. Charlotte followed. Christopher waited for her under a high ledge of a window. He pointed up as she approached.

"What is it?" she asked, squinting.

"It's a nest," he said, jumping up and down as he spoke. "Look."

Charlotte tilted her head back. Sure enough, a new nest was balanced on the sill, but the ledge tilted down a little, making it a precarious spot for a home. She squinted. The swallows made their nests in the rafters of the barn, not outside.

"The birds keep flying around." Christopher stopped jumping.

Just then a robin swooped down with a wad of hair— probably horsehair from the barn—in its beak.

"Well, well," Charlotte said.

"Do you think there are eggs in the nest?" Christopher asked.

"Not yet, I hope." Charlotte shivered. "It's too cold. They usually don't get started until April." It had been a long time since she'd been on this side of the barn, but she suspected that Christopher patrolled it regularly and that he would know if there were eggs.

It didn't seem like there were as many nests around as there used to be when they had baby birds hatching from spring until August. It had been years since any baby birds had fallen from their nests—at least any that they'd found —but when the kids were little they had found a lot. Maybe that was the key to finding nests and birds—having children around to observe them. Several times they had tried to feed the baby birds with eyedroppers, but they'd never been successful.

"I'm going to keep an eye on it," Christopher said. "Me and Toby."

"Toby and I." Charlotte couldn't help but correct him.

"Just don't let Toby get too close." She was remembering another boy and another dog years ago. Pete had found a nest down in a willow tree by the creek, and one day their old dog Blue had reached the spot first and scooped a fallen bird into his mouth. She shuddered. It had taken Pete quite a while to forgive that dog.

Charlotte heard Snowflake cry from the barn. It was 4:30, and Sam wasn't home yet. He had said he was planning to go to the basketball game in the evening, but she expected him home to feed the calf first. Surely he wouldn't forget.

"I'm going to go get Emily," Charlotte said. "We'll eat as soon as we get back." She turned to walk back to the house but then spun around again. "Thank you for sharing the birds' nest." She patted Christopher's shoulder. He was too tall for her to pat on the head anymore.

THE ARROW ON THE HEAT GAUGE of the car crept up slightly as Charlotte drove into town, but not enough for her to be alarmed. She parked in front of Fabrics and Fun, and as she climbed from the car, she noticed Sam's car pulling away from the curb on the other side of the street in front of the pharmacy.

She called out, "Hello, it's me," as she entered Rosemary's shop and hustled to the backroom, hoping her sister-in-law would be spared a trip to the front to see if a customer had entered. She found Emily and Rosemary both huddled over the pattern instructions.

"I don't get it," Emily said.

"You have to press the interfacing first." Rosemary straightened up.

"How's it going?" Charlotte asked.

"Okay," Emily said.

"It's a difficult pattern; that's for sure." Rosemary took a step away from the table. "Emily, who were you trying to impress when you designed these?" Rosemary sighed.

Emily shrugged and began folding the pattern. "It's pretty though."

"It was the first time I saw it." Rosemary chuckled, and for a second she looked like her old self, but then she grew serious again. "I have to admit, I'm a little tired of looking at it already. And to think we have two more to finish."

That didn't sound like Rosemary. Charlotte placed the cover over the machine. "Are we taking this home, Em?" she asked.

"May I come back tomorrow?" Emily asked, turning toward her great-aunt.

"Sure." Rosemary's face was tense; she seemed tired. "I'll be busier, hopefully, but you can make some more progress on Michelle's dress, at least."

"Are you feeling okay?" Charlotte asked her sister-in-law as Emily swung her book bag over her shoulder and headed through the door to the shop.

"I'm a little tired—like maybe I'm fighting a cold or something."

Charlotte patted her back. "Maybe you can get some extra sleep tonight."

"Maybe." Rosemary stopped at the counter by the cash register. "Hannah is coming by tonight, and we're going to firm up our plans for Dana's shower." She smiled. "It's going to be a lot of fun." She reached for Charlotte's hand and gave it a squeeze. "I'm so happy for Pete."

On the way home, as Charlotte was relishing the goodwill toward Pete, the heat gauge started to rise, going well past the midway mark. A minute later it soared to the red mark.

"Oh, dear," Charlotte said, pulling over to the side of the road to let the car cool down.

Chapter Sixteen

Sam hurried out the back door with the calf's bottle just as the phone began to ring. Grandpa was in his chair—surely he'd hear it.

He'd told Arielle that he'd pick her up after work—which was in forty-five minutes. He ran to the barn, slipping a little in the mud in the driveway. The basketball game had already started. He'd almost forgotten to come home to feed Snowflake—he'd kind of hung around the pharmacy for a while, pretending to be pricing cameras. Fortunately he remembered the calf with just enough time to buzz back to the farm.

He shoved through the barn door.

"Hey!" A voice boomed down from high in the barn. Maybe from the rafters. Sam tilted his head and squinted.

"Up here." It was Christopher, competing with Snowflake's bawling. Sam could make out his yellow sweatshirt. His feet were on a hay bale high on the stack and his hands were clutching a board below the window.

"What are you doing?"

"Trying to look out this window."

Sam hurried over to look up at his brother. "How many times has Grandma told you not to climb to the top of the hay bales?"

Christopher ignored him. "Grab the ladder by the tackroom door."

Sam obeyed his little brother, calling out, "Just a minute," to the calf. He staggered back toward the window, swaying the heavy ladder along. "Who uses this thing?" Sam asked, brushing his curls off his forehead.

"Uncle Pete. To change the light bulbs."

Sam looked up. Sure enough, the lights were high, higher than the window. He'd never noticed before. He spread out the legs of the ladder and stood it up next to Christopher so he could ease himself onto it.

"Why didn't you use this in the first place?" Sam asked.

"I didn't want to be obvious." He steadied himself.

"And a broken leg wouldn't be?"

Christopher ignored him and started climbing.

"Hey!" Sam yelled.

"I just have to check on something." Christopher climbed another rung.

"Come down."

He was level with the window now and leaned forward. "Grandma's right." He sounded disappointed. "There aren't any eggs in the nest."

"Hurry," Sam said. "I have places to go and people to see."

SAM OPENED THE GYMNASIUM DOOR for Arielle. He couldn't help but smile. Two weeks ago, he figured that he'd never have a chance with her again. And now here they were. "Where do you want to sit?" he asked.

"How about up there?" She pointed to the top of the bleachers, away from the student section.

His face grew warm as he guessed she didn't necessarily want to be seen with him. All of her friends thought he was a loser because he wasn't sure he wanted to go off to a four-year-college—and because he wasn't sure he wanted to go off to college at all.

That was what Arielle seemed to think too—at least what she had made clear when they broke up. People in Bedford were so conventional.

Sam frowned a little as they settled down on the top bleacher, leaning back against the concrete wall. "I really like watching basketball," Arielle said.

Basketball was such a Midwest sport, Sam thought. That and football. But at least basketball was fast-paced and easy to watch since it was all right there in front of the fans, not off at a distance like football.

"When do your games start up again?" Arielle asked.

"Mine?"

"Your soccer?"

"Oh," he said. "I'm pretty much done."

"Oh." She sounded concerned.

He shrugged. If he wasn't going to play college soccer there really wasn't much reason to keep up with it. And since his grades didn't seem good enough to get a soccer scholarship, then he might as well forget it. Soccer and college were the last things he wanted to talk about—or think about.

They were late for the varsity game. Two of Arielle's friends waved as they walked by, heading toward the student section. Arielle smiled and waved back. Bedford was ahead fifteen to eleven after the first quarter. As the buzzer rang to begin the second quarter, Uncle Pete and Miss Simons entered the gymnasium. They were talking intently.

"So what do you think of having Miss Simons for an aunt?" Arielle asked.

Sam gazed off into the distance. "It's weird," he said.

"Do you like her?"

"Yeah, she's cool."

"Are you in the wedding?" Arielle nudged him a little. Maybe. Or maybe she bumped him by accident.

"Yeah."

Arielle turned her head directly toward him. "And what are you?" She sounded annoyed.

"A groomsman." He looked at her.

"Oh," she said, and then, "Oh, look."

Uncle Pete and Miss Simons sat down a couple of rows ahead of them.

"Hey," Sam said, but Uncle Pete didn't turn around. He and Miss Simons were still talking.

At halftime, Arielle said she would be right back. As she walked down the bleachers, Uncle Pete turned around.

"Where'd you come from?" he said.

"I've been here the whole time," Sam said and then grinned.

Miss Simons said hello, and then she and Uncle Pete moved up one row and began chatting with Sam, asking him about school. Then Uncle Pete asked about the calf, but before he could answer, Uncle Pete turned to

Miss Simons and said, "He totally ruined the calf. I didn't think Sam had it in him to be a little mama like he's been, but the calf has bonded to him totally."

As luck would have it, Arielle came back up the stairs just then.

"We fed the calf the other night. Remember?" Miss Simons said to Uncle Pete.

"That's right." Uncle Pete looked like he was losing it.

"I adore that little calf," Arielle said. "He's the best."

"He's going to be the best hamburger around in another year," Pete said. "No one seems to get that."

"So he's still in the barn?" Arielle asked.

"Want to come out tomorrow?" Sam asked. "And see him?"

"Please do," Uncle Pete said, "'cause we're going to start charging, and it will go toward the calf formula." Uncle Pete turned around to watch the game, but in a couple of minutes he and Miss Simons had their heads together, talking again.

Sam caught the word *honeymoon* from Uncle Pete. And then Miss Simons said, "What? Three days?"

"Max," Uncle Pete answered.

Arielle nudged him. Sam shrugged.

Miss Simons scooted an inch away from Uncle Pete, but he kept talking. "I told you March was a bad time to get married."

"And June would be better?" she asked.

He shook his head.

"How about July?" She kept going. "August? September? October?"

He didn't answer.

"When, Pete?"

"December," he said matter-of-factly.

"You want to wait until December?"

"No," Uncle Pete said.

She stood.

"Dana."

"I'll be in my classroom. Working." She started down the stairs. Uncle Pete looked over his shoulder at Sam.

"Go after her," Arielle whispered loudly.

Uncle Pete started down the bleachers.

"I hope they work things out," Arielle said.

"They will." Sam pretended to concentrate on the game, but he was thinking that he needed to make sure and get married before he was old and clueless like Uncle Pete.

Chapter Seventeen

"What do you think is wrong with it?" Charlotte asked as she stepped out of her car and into the shed.

Bob shrugged. "Could be the radiator."

"Wouldn't you have noticed when you worked on the thermostat?"

His face turned red. "Not necessarily."

Charlotte gathered up her purse, and Emily collected her sewing things out of the trunk. "Did Sam go to the game?"

Charlotte noded. "He passed us, totally oblivious that my car was stopped on the other side of the road." No one had answered the house phone when she called so they had waited until the heat gauge was back in the middle and then drove home, straight into the shed, where she found Bob tinkering around on his truck.

"Maybe my car is just old enough to be falling apart all at once."

"It's not that old."

"Ten years."

"We can't afford to replace it."

Of course they couldn't afford to replace it.

He turned off the light and gave the door a yank. Charlotte scurried through before it started to close. "When's dinner?" he asked.

"Give me half an hour."

She had no idea where Pete was. Maybe he'd gone to the basketball game too. She knew that Dana liked to go to the sporting events to see her students play.

"Grandma." It was Christopher, standing in his socks at the back door. "There aren't any eggs in the nest."

"How do you know?"

He squirmed. "I checked."

She quickened her pace. "How?" She imagined him scaling the outside wall of the barn like Spider-Man.

"From the inside, from the window. Sam helped me."

"Oh." Charlotte reached the back door. "Sweetie, be careful. I don't want you doing gymnastics to check on that nest. Once the mama bird starts sticking around then you'll know she's sitting on her eggs. But that won't be for another month or two."

The half hour Charlotte thought it would take to finish making dinner turned into an hour. She'd forgotten to take the flank steak out to thaw. Bob couldn't find his reading glasses. She had to ask Emily three times to set the table and Christopher twice to unload the dishwasher. Finally they sat down to eat and Bob said grace. It had been a long day and Charlotte was ready for a nice meal.

AS CHARLOTTE CINCHED her bathrobe, Lightning rubbed against her leg, her brown head upturned.

Charlotte opened the back door, and the cat slinked outside. The morning was cold and crisp, another good day for plowing, even though it was a Saturday. There was no such thing as a five-day workweek on a farm. As she listened to the coffeemaker burble, Pete walked across the lawn with a bottle in his hand. Why was he feeding the calf? Pete had enough to do without playing nursemaid. He should leave Sam to do it now that it didn't matter how attached the calf was to him.

A minute later Pete entered the kitchen, bringing in the icy scent of the morning with him. "Sam left this in the barn," Pete said, tossing the bottle into the sink. "And the calf is frantic out there. Did he get a bottle last night?"

Charlotte thought he had but wasn't sure. "I think so," she answered.

Pete picked up a clean bottle from the counter.

"Let Sam do that." Charlotte took two mugs from the cupboard.

Pete spun around. "Where *is* Sam? Is he here? Ready and rarin' to go?"

He certainly seemed to be in a mood.

"Pete." Charlotte poured coffee into the cups. "What's the matter?"

He leaned against the counter. "Nothing." He sighed. "Everything."

"Like?" Charlotte put the cups on the table.

"Dana expects a big ol' honeymoon. Her mom expects a big ol' wedding. I expected a nice little celebration and a weekend trip. I found a cottage, part of a bed and breakfast, near Brownville." Pete followed Charlotte to the table.

"I thought once I figured out the rehearsal dinner and the honeymoon, I would be off the hook."

Charlotte sipped her coffee. The truth was, nothing felt simple anymore. Take today, for instance. She needed to take Emily in to Rosemary's, do the grocery shopping, buy a shower gift for Dana, and have Christopher help her clean out the chicken coop since Emily would be gone most of the day. She stood and grabbed the notebook from under the telephone on the desk. As she started to flip to a clean page, she noticed a phone number in Christopher's handwriting and a note that read, "Uncle Pete. Call this number. It's important."

"Pete," she said, "did you see this?" She slid the notebook across the table to him.

"It's that same number I tried the other day. Must be some marketer—or a scam."

"Or maybe something about the wedding? Maybe your tux?"

"It's not a Harding number."

She turned the notebook back around. "It's a River Bend number. The prefix is the same as Bill's office."

"Oh." Pete stood and grabbed the phone. "Maybe I'm late on the deposit for the rehearsal dinner." He started to dial.

"It's too early to call anyone," Charlotte said, glancing at the clock above the table.

Pete shrugged. "Maybe their machine is on."

It seemed to take a long time for the call to go through; then, just as Pete stepped toward the wall as if he were going to hang up, Charlotte heard him say, "Oh, hello." And then,

"This is Pete Stevenson. I had a message to call this number." He paused. "Yeah, I know it's early. Sorry." Then another pause as Pete's face fell. "You're kidding. You closed?"

He hung up the phone and turned to Charlotte and said, "The Riverside Inn went out of business."

"Oh, dear!"

Pete sank back down into his chair. "What do I do now?"

Charlotte reached out and patted his arm. "We'll figure something out." But she didn't feel so sure. It was less than two weeks until the wedding.

"HOW'S THE MOTHER of the groom?" Rosemary asked as Charlotte hauled Emily's sewing machine into the back room.

"Perplexed." Charlotte swung the case onto a table as Emily began pulling pieces of Michelle's dress from a bag. "The rehearsal dinner venue just went out of business."

"Goodness." Rosemary's hand flew to the side of her face. "That's terrible."

Charlotte nodded. "And everything seems to be booked."

"What about the Goldenrod B and B?"

"They're booked that night, and besides, that's where the reception is."

"Oh, that's right," Rosemary said. "Well, you could always have it out at the farm."

Charlotte chuckled. "Oh, I don't think that would go over very well." There was no way her shabby farmhouse would meet with Bonnie Simons's approval, not for the rehearsal dinner anyway. The engagement dinner had been one thing—but even then Charlotte sensed Bonnie's judgmental attitude.

"Sure it would. Pete and Sam could move the furniture from the family room out into the barn."

Charlotte cringed.

"And you could rent tables—it could be a regular restaurant setting."

Charlotte shook her head.

"Hannah, Mel, and I could help with the food."

"Mel! I hadn't thought of asking if we could have it at Mel's Place," Charlotte said. "Rosemary, you're a genius."

Her sister-in-law smiled. "Well, I'm glad you think so."

Charlotte nodded. "I'm going to go ask her right now before I head back to the farm." She turned and gave Emily a quick hug. "Call out to the farm when you're done." Charlotte bit her tongue to keep from saying anything about working hard or getting a lot done. It didn't do any good to pressure Emily, but all of them would feel a whole lot better once the dresses were completed.

She hurried past Pete's truck, which she'd driven into town, and headed down the sidewalk toward Mel's Place. Hopefully Bob would get her car going again today. As she pushed through the door, Ashley stepped out of the kitchen and greeted Charlotte.

"Hi, Ashley. Is your mom around?"

"She's across the street at the post office. She'll be right back. Would you like a cup of coffee?"

Charlotte graciously declined and said she'd hurry over

to the post office. On her way out the door she noticed Bonnie Simons going into the flower shop. *Whew, that was close.* Pete probably hadn't even thought of Mel's Place as an option. Melody didn't do many events, but the café would work—and it would be much better than Heather Creek Farm.

Charlotte ducked across the street and nearly collided with Melody as she came out of the post office.

"Charlotte!" Melody said, reaching out with a hug. "Where's the fire?"

Charlotte chuckled. "Well, the place didn't burn down, but it might as well have."

"What are you talking about?"

Charlotte explained what had happened. "So, any chance you have March 27 available?"

Melody's face fell. "I have a birthday party booked that night."

Charlotte gave her friend a hug and told her not to worry about it; they would find something.

"I could still help with the food," Melody said, "make some appetizers, salads. That sort of thing."

Charlotte thanked her and hurried on to Kepler's Pharmacy to pick up a card for Dana's shower.

IT WAS NEARLY NOON by the time Charlotte finished the grocery shopping; an icy rain had started so she loaded the bags into the cab of the truck instead of the back. She scooted into the driver's seat and heard someone call her name just as she started to pull away from the curb.

She turned around. Bonnie Simons was walking across the parking lot toward the truck. Charlotte started to get out, but Bonnie opened the passenger door first. A bag of groceries began to tilt, and Charlotte lunged for it, but she was too late. The bag crashed to the asphalt, right at Bonnie's feet.

"Oh, dear," Bonnie said.

Charlotte jumped from the truck and hurried around to the other side. Bonnie was crouched over the already wet bag and the dampening cardboard boxes of crackers, oatmeal, and croutons. A couple of cans of tomato paste had rolled beyond her.

"Oh, dear," Bonnie said again.

"No problem," Charlotte said, picking up the cans.

Bonnie stood, the wet bag in her hand. "I just wanted to talk with you about the rehearsal dinner. I just heard from a friend that the Riverside Inn has closed."

Charlotte tried to smile. "We have some ideas; we're working on it."

"So you knew but didn't tell us?"

"Oh, no." Charlotte pushed the groceries back into the truck and slammed the door. The rain started to come down harder. "We just found out this morning."

"Oh." Bonnie pulled her hood onto her head. "What ideas do you have?"

"Well, Melody said she can help with the food."

Bonnie smiled. "Actually, Mel's Place would be just fine."

"Oh, we can't actually have it there," Charlotte said. "She has an event that night."

Bonnie's eye began to twitch.

"But don't worry. We'll come up with something."

"What about at your house?"

"Our house." Charlotte stepped back. "Oh, I don't know," she said. "It's not really—right."

"Well, sure it would take some work." Bonnie's eye twitched again. "Well, let me know what you decide—ASAP, please."

CHARLOTTE GRABBED THE WET and torn bag of groceries and clasped it tightly as she walked toward the house. She eased in through the back door and tiptoed across the kitchen floor to the counter, hoping not to track in any mud. "Sam! Christopher! I need help bringing in the groceries."

Sam slid into the kitchen in his socks, the phone to his ear. "It's Emily," he said. "She wants to talk with you."

Charlotte took the phone as she pulled the boxes out of the bag and headed to the pantry. "Are you ready so soon?" she asked.

"Something's wrong with Aunt Rosemary," Emily whispered.

"What?"

"She sounds like she's drunk."

Charlotte stopped walking. "What do you mean?"

"It's not like she's been drinking, but her words are all slurred."

"Emily, is anyone else in the shop?"

"No."

"Okay. Call 911."

"I told her I was going to do that, but she says she's fine."

"Let me talk to her."

Rosemary came on the line a second later. "Charlotte, I don't know what Emily's talking about. I'm just a little tongue-tied is all."

"How about if you go to the Bedford Medical Center—just to get checked out?"

"I suppose I could drive myself," Rosemary said.

"No." Charlotte thought for a split second. "I'll find someone to take you. And I'm on my way into town."

Charlotte dialed Pastor Nathan's house, but he was out in the country on a visitation. Next she dialed Dana's number. She said she would hurry right over.

Relieved, Charlotte started back out to the truck. Rosemary didn't seem to share the high blood pressure and diabetes that her brother Bob had to deal with; at least Charlotte didn't think so. Actually, she seldom talked about medical concerns with Rosemary. For all she knew, she hadn't been to a doctor in years.

When Charlotte arrived at the medical center, she heard Rosemary's and Dana's laughter before she turned the corner into the waiting room.

"How are you?" Charlotte asked.

"Just fine." Rosemary held a can of cola in her hand. "I must have just needed a little pick-me-up because Dana gave me this to drink." She raised the can. "And I'm feeling much better."

"They drew blood for some tests," Dana explained.

"Already?" Charlotte hadn't sped into town but she'd come right in.

"They just finished," Rosemary said. "It's a slow Saturday

afternoon here at the medical center. Dr. Carr said a virus is going around, and I probably have that."

"Is Emily still at the store?" Charlotte sat down next to Rosemary.

"I'll go hang out with her." Dana stood.

"Thank you," Rosemary said, taking Dana's hand.

Dana patted Rosemary's shoulder and said she would see her soon.

"Tell Emily I'll be there in a little bit," Charlotte said.

A half hour later, Dr. Carr called Rosemary back to an examination room, and Charlotte tagged along. "I haven't seen you for a while," he said, flipping through her chart.

"I haven't had any concerns," Rosemary said.

He smiled. "I want to do another blood draw Monday morning, a fasting blood draw. First thing. And I'll have the results of the testing we're doing today then." He crossed his arms. "I'm sure this is just a virus, but you're at the age where you need to have regular checkups—cholesterol, blood sugar, all of that." He headed to the door. "You can make the appointment on your way out."

Rosemary stood and stretched. "I'm fine, really," she said.

Charlotte picked up her purse. "But you'll have the tests done Monday morning? Right?"

"Oh, I hate to close the shop again."

"You won't have to. It's just a blood draw. You'll be done in plenty of time." Charlotte led the way out of the examination room and stopped at the front desk.

Rosemary let out a big sigh and then said, "I need to make a lab appointment for Monday morning."

Chapter Eighteen

Monday afternoon Charlotte drove Pete's truck down to Hannah's to join her friend on a walk. The drizzly rain that had fallen all morning stopped just as Charlotte turned into the Carters' driveway, and the sun peeked out from behind the gray fluffy clouds.

Charlotte started to knock on Hannah's back door but before her knuckles connected with the wood on the screen door, Hannah boomed out a "Come on in!" and Charlotte stepped into her friend's kitchen.

"I'm just finishing up the cheesecakes for the shower tomorrow." Hannah flung her hand wide, motioning toward the three chocolate cheesecakes on the counter.

"Oh, my," Charlotte said. "They look beautiful."

"I'll just add the raspberry topping tomorrow before the shower." Hannah untied her apron as she spoke. "How about that walk? I sure could use some fresh air. And some exercise." Hannah grabbed her jacket by the back door, and they headed out across her lawn toward the creek, ducking under the budding willow trees.

The muddy water was running high. On the far bank, a robin pecked at the ground; it grasped a night crawler in its beak one second and then was gone the next. It flew upward, past a blossoming wild forsythia. Beyond that a patch of heather grew. No wonder Bob's ancestors had chosen to settle along the creek.

"Doesn't it seem early for the robins to be back?" Charlotte commented.

"It's the middle of March."

Charlotte thought for a minute, breathing in the sweet scent of the damp earth. It was March 16 to be exact. Christopher's birthday was coming in two more days. She gasped. She added *wrap the gifts* and *make a birthday cake* to her mental to-do list. She would have him choose what he wanted for dinner.

"What have you decided about the rehearsal dinner?" Hannah stepped ahead on the narrow trail.

"We haven't decided for sure." Pete had asked her last night if they could just have it at the farm. He said Dana was fine with it, and so was Bonnie. In fact Bonnie told Pete that she saw it as their only option.

"Well, I'd be happy to help. I can make desserts, rolls. You name it."

"Pete said he would barbecue; he's determined to have a steak-and-potato dinner." Charlotte smiled to herself. "To counteract the dainty food at the reception," was what he'd said, but she wasn't going to repeat that. "I'm just not sure," Charlotte added.

"What's your biggest concern?"

The trail widened, and Hannah slowed for Charlotte to walk beside her again.

"Oh, I don't know." Charlotte concentrated on keeping up with Hannah's long gait.

They walked in silence for a minute as Charlotte thought about what she would need to do to pull off the dinner. There was no getting around the fact that the interior of her house had grown shabbier in the last couple of years. She'd intended to paint the dining room and family room during the winter—but hadn't.

"Really," Hannah said, "it's just a dinner, one that's just a little bigger, really, than the holiday meals you pull off so flawlessly."

"I'm not worried about the dinner. It's the house I keep thinking about."

"The house?" Hannah looked at Charlotte with a puzzled look.

"It needs work." Even though she didn't allow the children to eat in the family room, the couch was stained. The carpet, which had already been quite old when the kids came to live with them, was now very worn. The walls were faded, and the woodwork could also use another coat of paint.

"Your house is fine. Besides, this is about being hospitable, right? And about celebrating Pete and Dana's marriage."

Charlotte knew her friend was right, but she still felt uneasy about hosting such a big event. She could clean the carpets and wash the woodwork. The boys could help with the scrubbing, and she could hire a crew to clean the carpets. She'd have to see about the painting.

"It will all work out," Hannah said. "Right?"

Charlotte nodded and said, "Right." But her voice was weak as she said the word. It felt like a setup for a lot of unmet expectations.

CHARLOTTE PARKED PETE'S PICKUP alongside Bob's and checked inside the shed. The hood of her car was up, and Bob was bent over the engine.

"How's it going?" she called out.

He straightened up, bumping his head on the hood. "Ouch." He stepped away, taking off his cap and rubbing his head. "I just put in a new thermostat; that discounted one I bought wasn't any good." Bob rubbed his hands together. "Rosemary's in the house."

Charlotte glanced out at the driveway. Rosemary's car was parked on the other side of Bob's truck. "She's not working?"

"Nope." Bob pulled his cap down tighter on his head. "She said she needed a day off. But then she got bored." He chuckled.

As Charlotte walked toward the house, she rolled her shoulders, trying to let go of her stress, and thought about ways she could de-clutter for the rehearsal dinner. Moving some of the furniture out was a good idea. Maybe she could use a couple of long tables from the church if the youth group wasn't going to be using them that night. That would save some money.

The scent of brewing coffee welcomed her into the kitchen. Rosemary stood in the middle of the worn linoleum, her steel-gray hair like a stormy cloud around her head. "When do the kids get home?" she asked without bothering with a greeting.

"Anytime," Charlotte answered, slipping off her shoes. "How are you?"

"Ridiculous." Rosemary laughed. "I had the blood drawn. No big deal, right? But Dr. Carr didn't have the results back from Saturday like he thought he would, and I started to feel all out of sorts."

"Ill?"

"No." Rosemary chuckled. "Mental, as the kids would say. I started to feel worried and anxious. What if something *is* wrong with me?"

Charlotte put her arm around her sister-in-law. "What do you mean?"

"Who would take care of me?" Rosemary's voice was practically a whisper.

Charlotte tightened her hold. "We would, of course."

"You have enough to take care of."

Charlotte shook her head. "Don't even go there. You're tired. You've been doing too much. You just need to rest." She pulled two mugs out of the cupboard. "Give yourself some time." She poured the coffee.

"I hate to be under the weather right now. There are the dresses, the shower, the rehearsal dinner."

"No worries," Charlotte said. "Everything is coming together. Hannah and Melody are all set for tomorrow; they're going to take care of the decorations."

Rosemary rubbed the side of her face. "I know they can handle it." Her eyes grew teary. "Make sure and put me down for a German chocolate cake for the rehearsal dinner to make up for this, okay?"

Charlotte reached over and patted her hand. That was Pete's favorite cake. "Just rest up for the shower—and for helping finish up those dresses."

"I could hem Emily's now," Rosemary said. "I could do it by hand. Don't you think that would be all right?"

Charlotte nodded. And she could get started on washing the woodwork with the help of the boys, while Emily and Rosemary sewed. She had frozen a batch of stew two weeks ago; she'd pull out a bag of that for dinner.

WHERE HAD ALL the handprints come from? An hour later, after the kids had had an after-school snack, Charlotte scrubbed around the back door as Christopher scrubbed the wainscoting on the mud porch. "What do you want for your birthday dinner?" she asked him.

He shrugged, not turning around to look at her.

She knew his birthday was difficult each year, a day when he felt his mother's passing acutely.

"How about chicken and dumplings?" Charlotte suggested. "Or ham steaks?"

When Christopher first came to Heather Creek Farm all he wanted to eat were chicken nuggets and hot dogs; his taste in food had definitely expanded.

"You can choose," he said.

Charlotte wished he'd cooperate. She didn't have time to try to read his mind. Maybe she would make up a multiple-choice questionnaire for him.

She kept scrubbing, only stopping to check the stew every once in a while. The sewing machine purred away in the dining room; it sounded as if Emily and Rosemary were having a productive afternoon. The phone rang as Charlotte turned the burner down, and she expected Emily to answer it. After a moment it was obvious that Emily wasn't going to so Charlotte picked it up.

It was Bonnie Simons calling. "Hi, Char," she said. Charlotte winced. Only Bob and Rosemary still called her Char. "Fabrics and Fun is closed. What's going on? Dana told me about taking Rosemary to the medical center on Saturday, but no one said it was serious."

Charlotte explained that Rosemary just needed a day off.

"But I need some more lace for Dana's veil—I'm outside the shop right now."

"I believe—"

Rosemary stood.

"—she'll be back tomorrow," Charlotte said.

Rosemary reached for the phone and then said, "I'll be right there." She handed the phone back to Charlotte.

"She could have waited until tomorrow."

Rosemary smiled. "I've rested long enough." She draped Emily's dress over the chair she'd been sitting on. "Besides, the hem's all done." She kissed Charlotte on the cheek. "I'll see you tomorrow at the shower."

After Rosemary left, Charlotte picked up the dress and examined the hem. It wasn't bad, but the stitches were larger than Rosemary's usual fine work. It didn't matter because Emily still had to sew on the pleated edging, but Charlotte couldn't help but wonder what was really going on with Rosemary.

HALFWAY THROUGH DINNER, Pete and Dana came through the back door. "Any food left?" Pete boomed in his usual startle-the-whole-house voice.

Charlotte jumped to her feet. "Of course," she said,

happy to see the couple. She hadn't asked Pete how things were going with Bonnie staying at Dana's because she hadn't wanted to meddle. But it was good to see the bride and groom together, seeming more relaxed than they had been in a week or two. "Come sit down. I'll grab the plates."

"I've got them." Dana spoke in a quiet voice. "Pete, get the glasses," she said, pulling him back from the table.

Emily smiled.

"How's Aunt Rosemary?" Dana asked as she set the plates at the end of the table and pulled up a chair.

"Tired, but besides that she seems fine." Charlotte was pleased that Dana called Rosemary "Aunt."

"Is it going to be too much for her to host the shower tomorrow?" Dana's eyes glistened.

"Oh no." Charlotte shook her head. "Hannah and Melody have everything under control. And I think Emily will have Michelle's dress ready—right?"

Emily coughed and then said, "Sure." She smiled. "It won't be quite done, but enough for her to try on."

"Thanks, Emily." Dana buttered her bread slowly.

Pete shoved a spoonful of stew into his mouth and then said, "Mom, we have the rehearsal dinner all figured out, right?" Then he turned to Dana.

She held her hand up. "It's fine—whatever you've decided. You can tell Mom next time you see her."

AFTER THE DISHES were cleared away, Emily set up the sewing machine on the table and pulled Michelle's dress from the bag.

As she pressed on the pedal with her foot, she thought of Aunt Rosemary. Everyone had been asking her for help. Bonnie Simons. Aunt Anna. Herself. She pressed harder on the pedal. Maybe it had been too much. Maybe that's why she was so tired and out of sorts; everyone had been stressing her out.

Emily slowed as she neared the end of the seam and then startled when Sam yelled, "Boo!" into her ear.

She rolled her eyes at him.

"Boy, I'm glad that we don't have to make our tuxes."

Emily didn't bother to turn around.

"You've been working on these dresses for weeks now."

It felt like months.

"I hope they're paying you." He plopped down in the chair beside her.

Emily shook her head.

"Then why are you doing it?"

"Because—" She paused. "Because I want to help Miss Simons?" She was a little surprised that her answer came out as a question.

"And I appreciate it," Miss Simons said from the kitchen.

Emily blushed. "I didn't know you were still here."

"Pete and I were answering the questions for our premarital session with Pastor Nathan. The shower's tomorrow so we couldn't procrastinate as long as we would have liked."

"You procrastinate?" Sam had mock horror in his voice.

Miss Simons laughed. "Mum's the word, okay?" She had her coat in her hands and slipped it over her shoulders. "So, Emily, is everything going okay?"

"Sure. No sweat."

Emily stood as Uncle Pete came into the room. "Please don't sweat. We don't want to have to wash the dresses before the wedding." It seemed like he was in a better mood.

"Pete." Miss Simons buttoned up her coat.

Uncle Pete winked at Emily, and she smiled on the outside. Inside she was annoyed with Miss Simons. It was hard enough to be stressed about the dresses without everyone asking about them all the time.

Chapter Nineteen

Tuesday afternoon, Charlotte ran into town and stopped by the post office to buy stamps and then by Mel's Place to hire Melody to make appetizers and her killer broccoli salad for the rehearsal dinner. By the time she turned onto Heather Creek Road she had begun to feel anxious about the shower, which was starting at seven. She needed to get dinner cooked and everyone fed.

Hopefully Emily wouldn't be scrambling to get Michelle's dress ready for the fitting. Charlotte wanted things to go as smoothly as possible so they could arrive at the shower relaxed and able to enjoy themselves. She took a deep breath as she turned into the driveway of the farm —and then held it as she spotted Anna's Toyota next to the house. Charlotte parked her car and hurried through the back door.

"There you are," Anna called out as the door slammed. "We've been waiting."

"I didn't know you were coming."

"I tried to call several times; I left a couple of messages." Anna stood in the middle of the kitchen, bouncing Will up and down. He had a terrific frown on his face, and drool rolled off his lower lip. "I decided to take the girls out of school this afternoon and try to get some sewing done before the shower."

"Oh." Charlotte leaned against the kitchen counter.

"I thought you could hold Will while I do some sewing." Anna nodded toward her sewing machine on the table. Emily's was at the other end, still out from the night before. Charlotte hadn't asked Emily how late she'd stayed up because she'd decided she didn't want to know.

"Will's teething," Anna said, as if that explained everything.

"Where are the girls?" Charlotte poured herself a glass of water from the tap.

"Out in the barn with Bob, looking at a baby calf."

Charlotte nodded. That was a good place for them to be. "Let me pull something out of the freezer for dinner." She would have to defrost it in the microwave. "Then I'll take the baby."

AN HOUR LATER, Emily came shuffling through the door. She barely smiled at Will and only said a muffled hello to Anna. She collapsed into the chair at the end of the table and stared at her sewing machine. When Anna took a bathroom break, Emily moaned, "Why are they here?"

"Anna wanted to get some sewing done before the shower."

"Why is her stuff always more important than mine?"

"Emily, hush." Charlotte bounced the baby up and down on her knee as she sat at the table.

"How about the skirt? Is she still going to make it?"

"Emily," Charlotte said. "Stop it." Will began to fuss, and she stood up. "Where's Christopher?"

"He was taking his time walking from the bus stop—said he needed to check something behind the barn."

Anna came back and sank into her chair. "Will was up half the night," she said. "I'm so tired."

Charlotte couldn't contain the question she'd been wondering about all afternoon. "Is he coming to the shower with us?"

Anna looked confused. "Yes. No." She ran her hand through her hair. "Bill is coming to get him. And the girls."

"Oh, I thought the girls would come," Charlotte said. Will started to fuss again and she bounced on her toes to soothe him.

"It's too late for them."

"Will you be okay driving home by yourself?" Charlotte asked. She'd never seen Anna so out of sorts.

Anna nodded. "I'll be fine."

"When is Bill coming?"

"For dinner."

The microwave beeped and Charlotte checked on the pork chops. She was cooking for ten. She counted quickly. She had nine pork chops. Emily, of course, wouldn't have one, but the boys—men—would have to forgo seconds.

CHARLOTTE STOOD in the middle of the kitchen floor, swaying Will back and forth. Bill had been a fussy baby too, but he'd been her first. She felt for Anna. It was hard to deal with a baby who didn't want to be put down when he was your third and you were shuffling older children to and from school and activities with the baby screaming in his car seat the whole time.

The back door flung open and Christopher fell through. "Are Jennifer and Madison here?"

"Outside, with Grandpa."

Christopher dropped his backpack and hurried back outside.

Emily stood, stretched, and walked toward the refrigerator. "He's slobbering," Emily said, pointing at Will. "All over your hand."

Charlotte glanced down. Sure enough, drool was cascading over her fingers. She hadn't even noticed. She washed her hands, transferring the baby from one arm to the other, and then went to the refrigerator to pull out the leftover salad from the night before. She could add to it and make it work for tonight too. She opened the vegetable drawer and then swung a bag of lettuce toward Emily. Her granddaughter scowled.

"Then take the baby." Charlotte pushed Will toward her, and Emily's arms automatically opened.

Will gurgled, and Charlotte expected Emily to say something more about his drool, but she didn't. Instead her face lit up. "He's smiling at me, Grandma." Emily had been so fond of him as a newborn; it was nice to see her fussing over him again.

Charlotte nodded. "He's a sweet baby, really." But a lot of work, for Anna anyway. Someday Emily would understand.

"He kind of looks like Christopher did when he was a baby. Except Christopher had hair."

Charlotte stepped around to where she could get a look

at both of her grandchildren's faces. Will was grinning at Emily. Yes, there was a little bit of a resemblance to Christopher. Charlotte felt a pang at not having seen Christopher until he was two years old and then not again for years.

"Is it okay if I take him out to the barn?" Emily asked.

"What about Michelle's dress?" Charlotte washed her hands at the sink.

"It's almost ready. I'll come right back in."

That would give Charlotte time to make the salad. "Sure, sweetie. Then I'll hold Will when you come back in, and you can finish your sewing."

EMILY DID FINISH HER SEWING—while the rest of them ate. Bill seemed a little annoyed as he spoke over the sound of the sewing machine, but the rest of them were getting used to the little motor purring away as the presser foot raced over the royal blue fabric.

Charlotte jiggled Will on one knee as she listened to Bill talk about the economy of River Bend. He said the city council needed to tighten the budget, and then he laughed. "I know my job is safe," he said. "Since it's unpaid." He explained there had been talk the year before of paying the mayor a small stipend, but any notion of that had recently evaporated.

"Being a public servant is very important," Charlotte said.

Anna looked annoyed and stood, taking her plate to the sink and then returning, her hands held out for the baby. "I'll feed him; then he should sleep in the car."

Bill stood. "How about when I get home? Should he sleep then?"

"Your guess is as good as mine," Anna said. Then Charlotte thought she heard Anna whisper, "This teething stinks," although she couldn't really be sure; but when Emily's head jerked up Charlotte took that as confirmation that she'd heard right. She smiled as she cleared the table. It was nice to know Anna was human.

Pete drove down the driveway as Bill loaded the children into his car, and the women put on their coats, readying themselves for the shower.

Bill popped his head up from securing Will in his car seat. "How's the groom?"

"Tired." Pete swung his legs down from his pickup.

"Can't wait until that rehearsal dinner." Bill rubbed his hands together. "Shrimp kebabs, steak..."

"Mom didn't tell you?" Pete sauntered toward the car.

"Tell me what?"

"Well, no kebabs, but we'll still have steak." Pete slapped Bill on the shoulder. "Here."

"At the farm?"

"What about the Riverside Inn?" Anna asked, buttoning her wool coat.

"It went out of business."

"I haven't heard a word about that," Bill said. "And the owner is a client of mine."

Pete shrugged. "I talked to him bright and early Saturday morning. He said the place closed."

Bill was obviously disturbed, but he patted Pete on the shoulder and said how much he was looking forward to the wedding. "Let us know what we can do to help with the rehearsal dinner." He turned toward his wife. "Right, Anna?"

"Right," she said, with the same tone of sarcasm Emily used when she was stressed.

Bill ignored her and said to Pete, "How are you holding up?"

"*Moi?*" Pete had a bemused look on his face.

Bill nodded. He was serious.

"No one asks about the groom." Pete crossed his arms.

"Give us a minute," Bill said. He put an arm around Pete and started walking him toward to the barn. "I remember—" His voice trailed off.

Charlotte watched her sons for a moment, but Anna stepped around the car and called out, "Bill! Come on. The shower starts in twenty minutes."

Bill and Pete stopped, paused, and then headed back, still talking. Charlotte was sorry they didn't have much time together—but happy that Bill was encouraging his younger brother.

ROYAL BLUE CANDLES and bunches of daffodils decorated the dessert and gift tables in the fellowship hall. Charlotte waved to Hannah, Melody, Ashley, and Rosemary in the kitchen as they walked into the room.

"I hope you haven't overdone it today," she called out to Rosemary.

"I'm feeling fine. Absolutely," she said, but her face was still pale.

"We're making her sit down now," Melody chirped. She still wore a red apron with Mel's Place embroidered across the bib. She pointed to the circle of chairs.

"Come sit by us," Charlotte said to Rosemary. She, Emily, and Anna took their seats.

"How's your skirt coming along?" Rosemary asked Anna as she sat next to her.

Emily leaned forward.

"Oh, that. It's not," Anna said. "I don't have time to do Madison's and Jennifer's dresses, let alone something for myself. I found something in the back of my closet that will work fine."

Emily relaxed against her chair.

The room quickly filled up with women, including Bonnie and Grandma Maxie, who sat on the other side of Charlotte, along with Dana's cousin Michelle. Hannah directed Dana to sit in the chair reserved for the guest of honor.

Once everyone was seated, Hannah clapped her hands together and said she was going to say a blessing for Dana. "Dear Lord," Hannah prayed, "we thank you for old friends and new friends, for families and those who feel like family. Mostly we thank you for how you knit us all together." She prayed briefly for Rosemary and then in more depth for Dana, asking that God would give her the strength she would need to be a good wife and that he would bless her marriage with Pete.

The women all echoed the prayer with a resounding amen, and then Hannah directed them toward the dessert table. Bonnie cut in line behind Charlotte, Emily, and

Anna, dragging Michelle along with her. Grandma Maxie went to the back of the line, even though Charlotte asked her to join them.

"When do you want to do the fitting?" Bonnie asked Emily.

"Um." Emily turned toward Charlotte, her eyes wide.

"How about after the shower?" Charlotte answered.

Michelle nodded, her perfectly bobbed dark hair bouncing up and down. "Sounds like a good idea."

Bonnie's eye twitched a little. "Let's do it right after—I want to make sure it gets done."

The women sat in a circle, eating their cheesecake and truffle cupcakes and visiting. Charlotte leaned forward and chatted with Maxie. She was eighty-eight but looked to be in her seventies with her perfectly coiffed bun at the nape of her neck and her stylish rayon dress, which she wore beneath a black cardigan. "I'm enjoying having Pete around again," Maxie said, her eyes twinkling.

"Oh?" Charlotte hadn't realized that Pete and Dana visited Grandma Maxie very often.

"They come around in the evenings some," she said. Her voice dropped. "I think to get away from all the wedding planning that's going on at Dana's house now."

Charlotte smiled just a little and nodded. Bonnie asked Maxie's opinion about the blue candles, and Charlotte turned her attention to Anna. Mothers- and daughters-in-law. It was quite the experience. Grandma Maxie and Bonnie had always seemed close, but there were obviously things that Grandma Maxie kept quiet about. Anna commented about how delicious the hazelnut and chocolate desserts were and then whispered, "The cheesecake is a little dry."

Charlotte hadn't noticed. She took another bite. In fact, it was delicious. She simply smiled and finished her piece.

While Emily and Ashley cleared the plates, Hannah pulled out a stack of papers. "We're going to play a game," she said, and then grinned.

Charlotte stifled a groan. She had expected some kind of entertainment, from what Hannah had said, but she'd never been any good at shower games.

"It's a how-much-do-you-know-about-the-bride game." She passed out the papers and pens, and Charlotte looked at hers. There was a list of questions about Dana. Where was she born? Where did she go to grade school? Whom did she go to the prom with her junior year?

At least Charlotte knew that one. She wrote down, "Pete."

What is her favorite book? Her favorite movie? Her favorite color. The list went on and on. Suddenly, Charlotte felt like she didn't know her daughter-in-law-to-be at all.

"Are the mothers excluded?" Bonnie held her pen in midair.

Charlotte nodded quickly, making eye contact with Hannah.

"That's only fair," her friend said.

Charlotte folded her piece of paper, relieved.

"What about grandmothers?" Grandma Maxie asked.

"That's up to you," Hannah answered.

Grandma Maxie held her pencil up in the air. "Then I'm playing!" The women all laughed.

As the guests answered the questions, Charlotte listened carefully. Dana was born in Minot, North Dakota, and went to grade school in Harding. Now Charlotte remembered that coming up in conversation one time. She had moved to Bedford when she was thirteen. When she was in college her parents moved to Grand Island, but she had chosen to return to Bedford when she got a job at the school.

Everyone clapped when Emily, who was now sitting by Ashley in the back, answered that Dana had gone to the prom her junior year with Pete. But Grandma Maxie knew that too. Her favorite book was *Pride and Prejudice*, and her favorite movie was *Sense and Sensibility*. Dana blushed and interjected that her answer wasn't entirely fair—but it was true.

Charlotte didn't realize what a big Jane Austen fan Dana was. Michelle knew that Dana and Pete planned to live in Dana's house in town while their house was being built on the farm.

Anna leaned toward Charlotte. "I didn't know they were building. Does Bill know that?"

Charlotte nodded. She was certain Bill knew, that Pete and Bob had spoken to him about it. She crossed her arms and then self-consciously uncrossed them.

Anna quickly answered, before anyone else could, that Jennifer and Madison were the flower girls.

The last question was, how many children did Dana want? Emily shouted out ten. Bonnie called out one. Someone else said two. Then three. Then four. Hannah kept shaking her head. Finally Grandma Maxie said, "More than one and fewer than five."

Everyone laughed until Hannah said that was exactly the correct answer.

Not surprisingly, Grandma Maxie won the game. Dana stood and took the few steps to her grandmother, leaning forward and kissing her cheek. "Grandma Maxie, I can't imagine my life without you," she said.

Charlotte's eyes filled with tears as she stole a look at Emily, but her granddaughter had her head next to Ashley's and hadn't seemed to notice.

A little later, Dana opened her gifts: a set of embroidered dishtowels from Hannah, along with a card file with a collection of favorite recipes; a cookbook and a casserole pan from Melody; a picnic basket and blanket from the pastor's wife; and an apron from Rosemary.

Charlotte turned toward Anna. "Are you sure you're going to be awake enough to drive home? You can sneak out early if you need to. Or spend the night at our house."

Anna said, "Bill might not appreciate that when Will wakes up for his feeding."

"That's true. Go ahead then. I don't want you to get drowsy driving home."

Anna decided that leaving early was a good idea. She whispered her good-byes to Hannah and Melody, and then waved at Dana. As soon as the last gift was opened, Bonnie stood and motioned to Emily. "Michelle can try the dress on in the ladies' room," she called out.

"I'll go out to the car to get it," Emily said. Ashley tagged along.

Charlotte took the opportunity to thank Hannah, Melody, and Rosemary for the wonderful shower.

"But I didn't do anything," Rosemary said, still sitting in her chair.

Charlotte patted Rosemary's shoulder. The shower had been a huge success. She spoke with Dana next, commenting on all the beautiful gifts and offering to help carry them to the car. As she loaded her arms with boxes, she looked around for Emily. It seemed like she was taking a long time to come back in from the parking lot. Charlotte made her way through the outside door of the fellowship hall, carefully walking toward Dana's car. The dome light of her own car was on. "Emily," she said, "what's the matter?"

Emily stepped into the light. "I forgot the dress." She looked as if she had been crying. "I must have left it by the back door when we were all in a rush to leave. Or in the driveway."

"Oh, Emily." Hopefully it wasn't in the driveway.

"Would you tell Bonnie and Michelle?"

Charlotte shook her head. "No, honey. You go tell them. And schedule a fitting with Michelle for later this week—but keep in mind that she'll have to give more of her time to come back to Bedford for this."

Chapter Twenty

Emily pressed her nose against the window of Grandma's car as they traveled back out to the farm. Grandma drove slowly through the thick fog.

"I hope Anna made it home okay," Grandma said, not taking her eyes off the road. "And I hope Michelle's dress is safe inside the house." She gave Emily a quick smile and then jerked her attention back to the soupy darkness ahead of them.

Emily knew the dress wasn't in a bag in the driveway or by the back door. She had out-and-out lied to Grandma and then to Ashley too—a blatant, premeditated lie. She had left the bag beside the dining room table on purpose. She couldn't bear the thought of Michelle trying on her dress in front of Bonnie Simons, with Miss Simons standing close by.

She had imagined Michelle coming out into the fellowship hall and everyone closing in for the kill—um—the inspection. She imagined fingers grabbing at the fabric and mouths commenting about the color and texture. She imagined hands seeking the inside seams, eyes automatically measuring the seam allowances, gasps at the way the neckline puckered at one corner. She imagined the downturned mouths, the disapproving glances, the clucking tongues.

She couldn't face that, not in a million years. What in the world had possessed her to volunteer to sew anything for the wedding?

When she told Michelle and Bonnie Simons that she had forgotten the dress, Mrs. Simons had thrown up her hands, turned to her daughter, and said, "This is exactly the chaos I warned you about. Nothing goes right for this family."

Miss Simons had hurried to Emily's side and defended her—which made Emily feel horrible. But Mrs. Simons's comment, even though she didn't totally understand it, made her feel worse.

Grandma wrinkled her nose as she drove along, intent on the road. "When did you reschedule the fitting for?" she asked.

"Friday at five o'clock at Fabrics and Fun."

"Will Dana's mother make the fitting?" Grandma asked

"I don't think so," Emily answered, hoping her voice didn't give away her relief. "I think she had some other commitment."

Grandma glanced at Emily and then back at the road. She seemed a little suspicious, but Emily couldn't be sure. And she should be. Emily had specifically scheduled the fitting for Friday once she found out Bonnie Simons wouldn't be available.

They rode along in silence until Grandma turned onto Heather Creek Road. "What were we thinking?" Grandma bumped her forehead with her hand. "You should have called the house with your cell and asked Sam to check the driveway."

"I don't think I left the dress outside..." Her voice trailed off.

"I don't see the bag," Grandma said, slowly pulling into her usual parking place.

Emily got out of the car and jogged up to the house. She slipped through the door, made a motion of looking from side to side in case anyone was watching, and scurried into the dining room, snatching up the bag. She pirouetted around and stepped back into the kitchen. "Here it is." She smiled as Grandma came through the door. "Silly me. I left it in the dining room."

Grandma gave Emily one of her looks—her I'm-not-buying-your-story look—and then said, "Are the boys here?"

"In the family room." It was Christopher. He appeared in the doorway, wearing his pajamas and yawning.

"Where's Sam?" Grandma asked.

"In the barn, giving Snowflake his bottle." Christopher opened the refrigerator and grabbed the pitcher of milk. "And Uncle Pete went in to town to check out Miss Simon's loot."

"Christopher." Grandma opened the cupboard and retrieved a glass.

"Those are his words, not mine."

"What about Grandpa? Have you seen him?"

Christopher cocked his head. "Isn't he in bed?" Christopher poured his milk, sloshing a little onto the countertop.

"I don't think so. His coat isn't on its hook." Grandma went to the back door and called out. Then she came back into the kitchen. "His pickup isn't here. Where would he have gone?"

Emily grabbed her book bag from the mud porch. She still had an English essay to write. Plopping herself down at the table, she pulled out her notebook. It didn't have to be typed—just in legible handwriting. Next year she would have Miss Simons for English, except then she would be Mrs. Stevenson. That was going to be so weird. What if she was pregnant with her first of more than one and fewer than five children? Emily couldn't imagine; she shivered a little at the thought.

"Are you cold, Em?" Grandma asked. Toby began to bark, and Grandma hurried to the back door, but it was Sam, not Grandpa.

"I'm going to call Dana's and see if Pete passed Grandpa's truck going into town."

"Grandpa's in the shop," Sam said, shaking his head.

"What?"

"He's working on his truck. Said he's practicing to open a repair shop." Sam laughed. "He said I could be his business partner."

"Oh, dear," Grandma said, grabbing her jacket and marching out the door.

Emily settled back down and read the assignment: "Write a persuasive essay." She tapped the end of her pen against her chin. Her thoughts were interrupted by the phone ringing.

"Sam, would you answer that?"

No one responded.

"Christopher?"

Again, no answer.

Emily stood and lunged for the phone. It was Uncle Bill. "Well, at least *you're* home," he said. "What time did the shower end?"

She could hear Will crying in the background and Jennifer yelling, "Daddy!"

"About forty-five minutes ago."

"Thank goodness. Anna should be home any minute."

Emily wasn't sure what she should do. "Uh, Uncle Bill." She paused.

"Yes?"

"Aunt Anna left early."

"How early?"

She'd never heard Uncle Bill sound afraid before.

"Maybe a half hour."

"Then she should be here by now."

"Did you call her cell?" Emily asked.

"She didn't answer." Will's crying grew louder. "Let me talk to Mom, okay?" Uncle Bill sounded exhausted.

"She's out in the shed."

"Would you go get her?" His voice softened, and Emily could hear Jennifer yelling in the background again.

"I'll have her call you right back," Emily said, hanging up. She hurried into the family room, where Sam was hunched over the keyboard, typing away. "Go get Grandma," she said. "Tell her she needs to call Uncle Bill." Emily didn't mean to sound alarmed, but she must have because Sam looked up.

"What's up?"

"Anna isn't home yet."

"So?"

"She left the shower over an hour ago." Emily turned on her heels. What if something had happened to Aunt Anna? Her kids were so little. Emily's eyes filled with tears. She'd go get Grandma herself. Emily slammed through the back door and hurried across the lawn. The door slammed again behind her.

"Emily!" It was Sam. "What's going on?"

She turned. In the light from the landing she could see Christopher at the window.

"Go back to the computer!" Emily yelled. She reached the driveway, and from there she could make out Grandma and Grandpa, standing beside the pickup. She didn't want to scare them. There was no reason to be worried. Maybe Aunt Anna had stopped somewhere. No. She would go straight home to her baby.

"Grandma!" Emily shouted.

"I'm right here, Emily." Grandma stepped from behind the truck. "You don't need to yell."

"You need to call Uncle Bill. Aunt Anna isn't home yet."

"Well, it's not that late—" Grandma held her wrist up. "Oh, dear. She should be home by now. Did Bill say if it's foggy in River Bend too?"

Emily shook her head.

"Come on," Grandma said, putting her arm around Emily. "Let's go back to the house." She motioned to Grandpa, and he started to lower the shop door as they scurried out.

Sam stood in the middle of the lawn, but Christopher stepped away from the window when he saw Grandma.

"She'll probably have arrived by the time I call Bill," Grandma said. "Don't you think, Sam?"

He nodded.

Emily thought of that awful day when she got the horrible news about her mother. She shivered and swallowed hard. *Don't borrow trouble,* Grandma sometimes said.

"She was pretty tired," Grandma said as they reached the back door and followed Sam into the house. "Maybe she stopped for a cup of coffee."

"I don't think she would," Emily said. "I think she's the kind of mother who would hurry home."

"Well, mothers need to take care of themselves too," Grandma explained, taking off her coat. "So they can take care of their children." Grandma smiled at Emily as she reached for the phone. "Go ahead and finish your homework."

Emily sat down at the table and picked up her pen. Grandma stepped into the hall to talk, but Emily could tell from her tone that Aunt Anna hadn't arrived yet.

Sam stepped into the dining room with a questioning look on his face.

Emily shook her head as Christopher tiptoed into the dining room. "What's going on?" he whispered.

"Nothing," Emily answered, looking over her baby brother's head to her big brother.

"Something is." Christopher crossed his arms. "Who is Grandma talking to?"

"Uncle Bill," Sam answered.

"Did something happen? Are Jennifer and Madison okay?"

"It's Aunt Anna," Sam said.

Emily sputtered.

Sam continued, "She's not home from the shower yet."

"Oh." Christopher turned. "I'm going back to bed."

"We'll let you know what happens," Emily said, but Christopher was already on the staircase by the time she finished her sentence. She turned on Sam. "Why did you tell him?"

"Because it's the truth."

"But now he's going to worry."

Sam shrugged. "You're the most worried." He settled back down at the computer.

Emily tried to concentrate on her essay until Grandma came back in to hang up the phone. "I told Bill she was tired—that surely she stopped for a cup of coffee or something."

"But she's nursing. Remember? She's not drinking caffeine. And she didn't answer her cell phone."

"Honey, she might have made an exception as far as the caffeine. And she probably turned her phone off for the shower." Grandma paused for a minute, as if she'd forgotten something. Then she said, "I'm going to go pray with Christopher and tuck him in."

"Say a prayer for Aunt Anna."

Grandma turned back around. "How about if you and I pray right now?"

Emily paused and then nodded her head. "Okay."

Grandma stepped closer to Emily and bowed her head. "Dear Lord, we ask you to protect Anna and to return her to her family safely—and soon. Amen."

"Amen," Emily whispered.

Grandma gave her a quick hug and headed up the stairs, and then Emily jotted down a few ideas for her essay. It was supposed to be a persuasive piece. She needed to come up with an idea. Mrs. Thomas said they couldn't write about a political issue. She'd read plenty of those essays. She wanted them to choose something they felt strongly about from personal experience.

Emily held her pencil in midair. No one knew for sure what had caused her mom's accident. She might have swerved to miss an animal; that would have been like her. Or she might have fallen asleep. That was more likely because there hadn't been any skid marks. It was afternoon. It was warm. She'd worked late the night before and then gotten up early to get all of them off to school.

"Don't drive when you're tired," Emily said out loud as she wrote it down. That's what she would write about. It would have been better for Aunt Anna to have missed the bridal shower than for her to fall asleep on the way home.

Emily took a deep breath. She felt bad now for making a stink about Aunt Anna coming over so Grandma could help with Will while Aunt Anna sewed. Being a mom might be harder than Emily had thought. Maybe Aunt Anna needed more help. Will was really cute, but he seemed to make life difficult. Aunt Anna—or Grandma or whoever was holding him—only had one good arm to use when she was taking care of Will.

Emily tapped her cheek with the pencil eraser again. Maybe she should write an essay persuading people not to have kids at all. She thought that over for half a second and then said, "No," out loud.

"Pardon?" Grandma came back into the room just as the

phone rang again. She snatched it up before Emily had a chance to scoot her chair back. "Oh, good," Grandma said. She smiled at Emily, who sank back in relief.

Grandma was off the phone in record time. "She stopped and got herself a cup of tea. She said the fog had lulled her nearly to sleep and she needed a pick-me-up. She's fine."

Emily stood. "I'll go tell Christopher." She started through the family room, telling Sam the good news as she went.

"Told you so," he said.

Emily hurried up the stairs and eased Christopher's door open. His light was off. "Christopher," she said. He didn't answer. When her eyes adjusted to the light, she saw that he was asleep.

By the time she got settled at the table again it was ten o'clock. The sewing machine was still in the corner of the dining room. The bag with Michelle's dress in it was still against the wall. She concentrated on her essay for a moment. Mrs. Thomas had said to write about something they felt passionate about or something they wished they hadn't done. She wished she hadn't volunteered to make the dresses. If she wrote about that Mrs. Thomas might tell Miss Simons though.

She'd better stick with the don't-drive-when-you're-tired idea. She'd heard it could be as lethal as driving while drunk, but quicker to remedy. All it took was a nap or stopping for a cup of coffee or switching drivers.

Now she needed some statistics to back up her argument. "Sam," she called out, "I need the computer."

Chapter Twenty-One

Charlotte whipped the toothpick out of the double chocolate cake. "Done," she said triumphantly, grabbing the oven mitts as she glanced at the clock. She had an hour before the children would be home from school. That would give her plenty of time to ice the cake before dinner.

She set it on the cooling rack, and then turned her attention toward the gifts on the table. She'd picked up a new pair of jeans and a T-shirt in Harding a couple of weeks ago. She didn't know what Sam or Emily had gotten Christopher, but she had reminded them a few days ago so they wouldn't forget. Just this morning she'd picked up a carton of Whoppers, a card, and a discounted gift bag decorated with racecars at the pharmacy. Quickly she wrapped the gifts in tissue paper and slipped them into the bag.

"Bob," she called, "I need you to sign Christopher's card."

"I'm coming." He had his jacket and hat on.

"Where are you headed?"

"Out to the shed—I'm in the middle of tuning up my truck." He signed the card, poured himself a cup of coffee, and banged out the door with it.

Charlotte had a little time to do more cleaning before she started making fried chicken for Christopher's birthday dinner. She retrieved her bucket from beneath the sink and filled it with hot water, adding some cleanser. If she had any hope of painting the dining room walls, she needed to wash them first.

As it turned out, she had only washed one wall before she remembered that she hadn't given Snowflake his noon bottle. By the time she finished, the kids were home and she served them the frosted sugar cookies she'd made that morning especially for Christopher's birthday. Then Emily asked her to edit her English essay before she typed up the final draft and Christopher needed help with his math. By the time she frosted the cake, it was time to start dinner.

"AREN'T YOU GOING to eat with us?" Charlotte asked Pete as she plopped a massive spoonful of creamy mashed potatoes into a serving dish.

"Nah." He rubbed his elbow. "I'm going to go into town and eat with Dana before our pre-mar-i-tal coun-se-ling session." He grinned. "Bonnie is having dinner with Grandma Maxie tonight."

"It's Christopher's birthday."

"Oops," Pete said.

She'd meant to tell him last night, but in all the hubbub before—and after—the shower, she'd forgotten. She had been so relieved when Bill called to tell her Anna was safe and sound, that she had gone to bed before Pete got back from Dana's.

"I'll pick up something at the store, and give it to him later tonight," he said.

"Pete."

"I already told Dana I would have dinner with her."

Charlotte pursed her lips, trying to choose her words carefully. But Pete was out the door before she could figure out what to say. As she turned around she caught sight of Christopher lurking by the pantry door.

"So it will just be you and Grandpa, Sam and Emily and me for dinner?"

Charlotte nodded. Christopher leaned against the wall with a sad, distant look spread across his face.

"Could you call Emily and Sam to the table, please?"

He stared straight ahead.

"Christopher?" She touched his shoulder, and he jumped, his gaze falling to the floor. "Call your siblings, okay? And tell Grandpa it's time to eat."

CHARLOTTE WAS STACKING the dirty dinner plates when the back door swung open.

"Any food left?" It was Pete, followed by Dana.

"Of course," Charlotte said.

Pete cleared his throat. "Happy birthday, Christopher."

Dana echoed the greeting.

"I'll be right back," Charlotte said, taking the stack of plates to the kitchen. Pete followed and took two clean plates from the cupboard. "How come you're back?" Charlotte whispered.

"Dana was really upset. She said of course Christopher's

birthday was more important than dinner with her." He glanced at his watch. "We have time for a quick bite of dinner and some cake—then we need to head to the church."

Dana had settled into a chair next to Christopher, and he was smiling at her. She placed a gift on the table and then took the plate Pete handed her.

Sam was obviously getting restless, most likely eager to get on the computer.

"How's the calf doing?" Dana asked.

Sam's face reddened.

"Sam," Charlotte said, "did you check on him after school?"

He shook his head. "Can I do it right now?"

Charlotte said, "No. Wait until after we have cake. And give him his evening bottle at the same time."

Now he was really fidgety. Charlotte was a little surprised when he began talking. "Snowflake is doing fine. I can't believe how much he's growing. And he started to eat alfalfa." Sam sounded like a proud parent. "I always thought it was stupid when people said how quickly babies grow up, but now I get it." He grinned.

After Christopher blew out his candles, he began opening his gifts, first the one from Bob and Charlotte and then a drawing pad and pen from Emily.

"Hey, bud," Sam said. "My gift is an ice cream sundae at Jenny's Creamery, okay? Whenever you want."

"How about Friday?"

Sam grinned. "You've got it."

Christopher began to tear the paper off the gift Dana had given him.

"That's from Pete and me," she explained.

Everyone around the table smiled, including Pete. "Having a wife—almost—is really coming in handy," he said.

Dana nudged him good-naturedly.

"That's what Sam needs," Christopher said.

"I beg your pardon?" Charlotte said.

"You know, so he'll remember birthdays." Christopher held up a paperback copy of *Robinson Crusoe*. "Cool," he said and then thanked Dana.

"It's about a guy who gets marooned on an island," Sam said.

"It's one of the first novels ever written," Dana said, taking a bite of cake.

Christopher examined the book. "It doesn't look that old."

Dana laughed. "Well, this is a newer copy. But it was written in the seventeen hundreds. Long before *Treasure Island* was written. They're both classics though. I think you'll like it."

Christopher placed the book on the table. "Thank you." He smiled at Dana and then gave Pete a quick smirk. "Thanks, Uncle Pete."

Pete rubbed his hands together. "Well, you know it is one of my favorite books—just kidding." He stood. "We've got to get going."

Christopher stood and hugged Dana quickly and then hugged Pete. He didn't say a word, but Charlotte sensed that his actions had deep meaning. Having a woman in the family close to the age his mother would be, had she lived, might do Christopher good. Charlotte felt the familiar stab of tears in her eyes at the thought of Denise.

"Christopher," she said, thinking that if she spoke she wouldn't cry, "only one more year, and you'll be a teenager."

"Yep," he said.

"Poor Mom," Pete groaned, and everyone laughed.

The tears won and Charlotte couldn't speak at all as Christopher turned to hug her.

SOON AFTER PETE AND DANA LEFT, Bob slipped into his coat. "I'm going in to town," he said.

"What for?" Charlotte looked up from the sink where she was scrubbing the pots and pans and Emily was drying them. He never went into town this late—it was almost eight.

"I thought I'd visit Rosemary, see how she's doing."

"Do you want me to come along?" She slipped a pan into the rinse water, and brushed a stray hair off her forehead with her wrist.

"Stay here with the kids," Bob said. "I won't be long."

"Grandpa." Emily dried her hands on the dishtowel. "May I go with you?"

Before Charlotte could intervene, Bob answered, "Yes." He looked so pleased, Charlotte didn't want to discourage it.

Still, she said, "Em, what about your homework? And the sewing?"

Emily hung the towel on the hook. "I'm done with homework, and if I sew one more stitch tonight I'm going to start screaming."

"Well, call first. What if she decided to go to bed early?"

Chapter Twenty-Two

It had been a long time since Emily had gone anywhere with Grandpa. Each time she did, she remembered how quiet he was. They rode along in silence, the starry night hanging over them like an umbrella. Emily stargazed out the window.

Grandpa stopped in front of Aunt Rosemary's little Cape Cod cottage. As they started up the stairs, the front door swung open.

"Like I said," Aunt Rosemary called out, "you really didn't need to come into town. I'm fine. But it's nice to see you."

Emily followed Grandpa, and they all settled in the tiny living room with the camelback sofa and the antique lamps.

"I'm feeling much better," Aunt Rosemary said. "I saw Dr. Carr today. He thinks I had a touch of the flu; that's why I was feeling poorly. But my blood work came back, and my cholesterol is a little high. We'll see if I can lower it with diet and exercise, and then, depending on how that goes, he might start me on some medicine." Rosemary sat on the edge of her chair. "And my blood pressure is high, so I have to take medicine for that."

Emily yawned. There was nothing worse than old people sitting around talking about their health.

"I was thinking." Aunt Rosemary turned her attention to Emily. "Why don't you plan to come and sew all day on Saturday? We probably can finish those dresses just like that."

"That would be great," Emily said. "And remember I'm coming on Friday, to do Michelle's fitting."

"That's right," Aunt Rosemary said. Emily was pretty sure she'd forgotten.

"Well, well," Aunt Rosemary said, facing Grandpa again. "We certainly are getting old, aren't we, big brother?"

Grandpa rubbed the top of his head. "Speak for yourself, little sis." He grinned.

"When Dad was your age, he'd turned over the farm to you. Isn't it about time you give it up?"

"I've turned a lot of it over to Pete." Grandpa twirled his hat in his hands.

"But what about the rest?"

"The rest? If I turned it all over to Pete he'd be off to Harding to buy a new tractor. And he'd probably forget to seed. And the equipment wouldn't be running."

Emily perked up.

"Now, Bob," Aunt Rosemary said, "do you think you had it all together when Dad turned the farm over to you?" She laughed. "Remember the time you planted barley instead of wheat? Or the time the brakes went out on the farm truck?"

Grandpa stopped twirling his hat.

"Or the time—"

"Rose."

"—you got mixed up on the vaccines—"

Grandpa stood.

"Oh, come on, Bob. I'm just teasing."

Emily stared at Grandpa. Had he really done all those things?

"My point is, you need to give Pete some slack. You've been hovering over him all these years."

"It's step-by-step, Rosemary. I'll know when it's time to completely turn over the farm to Pete—and we're not there yet." He took a step toward the door. "I'm glad you're feeling better."

"Come on. Give me a hug." Aunt Rosemary stood, and Grandpa enveloped her in his arms. Emily wondered if she and Sam would be like Grandpa and Aunt Rosemary someday. Maybe Sam would have a wife that Emily would be close to. Who knew? She shook her head. Honestly, she couldn't begin to imagine fifty years from now.

Grandpa hugged Aunt Rosemary a little tighter. "I'm really glad you're feeling better. Take care, okay? And let Charlotte know if you need anything."

Aunt Rosemary chuckled and slapped Grandpa's back. "Charlotte has plenty to do without looking after me too."

EMILY CONCENTRATED on homework Thursday after school, dreading the dress-fitting session the next day. And then all day Friday she dreaded it even more. After school Sam drove her to Fabrics and Fun. When he stopped the car, she slung her book bag over her shoulder and then walked to the back of the car and popped open the hatch while Christopher scurried out from the back seat, ready to go to Jenny's Creamery. Both he and Sam started down the street. "Hey," Emily called out.

"Hey, what?" Sam looked over his shoulder as he walked.

"Help me, would ya?" She pulled out the bag with Michelle's dress and pointed at her sewing machine.

Sam slouched back to the car while Christopher hopped around on the sidewalk. He frowned.

"Boy, you're grumpy." She led the way across the sidewalk and opened the door.

Sam put the machine down just inside the door.

Emily cleared her throat.

"You're not helpless," Sam sneered.

Emily flexed her arms. "Of course I'm not, but that doesn't mean you can't help me out."

He grunted and pushed on the door.

"Have fun at the ice cream shop."

"We'll definitely have more fun than you," he said. And then he grinned as he stepped out of the store.

She called out, "It's just me," hoping to save Aunt Rosemary a trip to the front of the store, but then she noticed her aunt in the corner, looking over paperwork.

"Aunt Rosemary?" Emily said.

"Oh, hi there. Is school out already?"

Emily nodded.

"Well," Aunt Rosemary said, "make yourself at home. I'm doing the books—and need to get this done today. I'll help you with your sewing tomorrow."

Emily thanked her and kept on going to the back room. She had over an hour to start working on Amber's dress before Michelle and Miss Simons arrived. Just as she pressed the sewing machine pedal the front door of the shop buzzed, and a minute later Bonnie Simons came sashaying into the back room. "I need a tiny bit more lace," she said, "and I just thought I'd have a check-in with you before I head over to Harding for my appointment." She carried the wedding-planning clipboard in her hand.

Emily stood and picked up Michelle's dress, pulling it out of the bag by its hanger. "Everything is fine."

Bonnie Simons stepped closer to the dress. "My, it certainly is blue, isn't it?"

Emily tried to smile.

"No wonder Pete didn't want a tie and cummerbund to match." She sighed. "Well, this is what Dana wanted, I guess." A moment later the woman waltzed back out of the room.

A few minutes later Aunt Rosemary came in. "I'm going to take my paperwork home," she said. "I turned the sign—but you can stay." She had a key in her hand. "This is an extra. Turn off the lights and lock up when you leave."

Emily took the key and squeezed her fingers around it. "Is it okay if I come tomorrow?"

"I'm planning on it," Aunt Rosemary said. "I'm going to get some extra sleep tonight." She sighed. "I'm still feeling a little under the weather."

She gave Emily a little wave as she headed back through the shop.

Emily began to sew again. It was nearly dark outside, and she didn't like being in the shop alone. When the sewing machine was whirring away, she imagined hearing things. Someone out back. A screech along the window.

She took her foot off the pedal—all was silent—so she started sewing again.

When she stopped again, she heard a knocking and walked quickly into the shop. Both Michelle and Miss Simons were pounding on the door.

Emily dug the key from the pocket of her jeans and quickly unlocked the door.

"I was afraid you weren't here," Miss Simons said, leading the way through the shop.

"I guess I was concentrating too hard." Emily hurried to the back room and snatched up Michelle's dress, holding it above her head so that it hung straight from the hanger.

"It's gorgeous." Miss Simons said, holding her hands together.

Michelle nodded, taking the hanger.

"You can change in the restroom." Emily suddenly felt jittery. Miss Simons liked the look of the dress, but what if she nitpicked over the little stuff? She pulled the cut-out shawl from the stack of fabric beside her sewing machine and held it up. "We just need to choose the fringe; these will be really easy to make."

"Let's look now." Miss Simons followed Emily back into the shop, to the far wall. There wasn't much of a selection. There was only one fringe that was royal blue; luckily it matched the fabric and the trim on the dresses.

"The shawls will be perfect," Miss Simons said. "They're going to add to the old-fashioned feel of the wedding. It will be great."

"Lots of 'something olds,'" Emily said, "including Melody's dress."

"Well, Melody's gown isn't that old."

Emily's eyes must have gone wide, because Miss Simons laughed and then said, "I guess you're right. It is old. I'm just getting a late start." Then she sighed.

Emily was relieved when Michelle called out, "Hey, where'd you guys go?" And then there she was, standing in the archway, in her socks and the blue, blue dress.

"Oh, it looks so pretty on you," Miss Simons said. And it did.

"Come stand on a chair." Emily hurried to her sewing machine and grabbed her pincushion. "Where do you want the hem?" she asked Miss Simons.

"Midcalf." She stepped back. "Emily, you've done such a good job." And then quietly she said, "I can't wait to tell Mom."

Emily stuck a few pins in her mouth. She didn't want to tell Miss Simons that her mother had already seen the dress—and hadn't sounded positive. She didn't want to ruin the fact that she felt like a real seamstress again. She could almost imagine having a shop someday. Not in Bedford, but maybe in a midsize city, after she was done in New York, of course. She could design and sew and help other people with their—

"Ouch!" Michelle jerked away, nearly toppling off the chair. "You got me."

"I'm sorry," Emily muttered through the pins in her mouth, glancing up at Miss Simons. But she hadn't noticed. She was slumped in a chair, clutching the bolt of fringe in her lap.

After they left, as Emily waited for Grandma to pick her

up, she called Ashley on her cell. She was feeling bad about tricking Miss Simons and Michelle into doing the fitting today instead of the night of the shower, and that had made her think about not admitting to Ashley that she had cut out the sleeves wrong on her own dress too.

"Hey," Emily said when Ashley answered. They chatted for a minute. Emily told her about the fitting and then said she needed to tell Ashley something about the evening she'd been there cutting out Michelle's dress.

"You already apologized," Ashley said.

"I know. But I didn't tell you that Aunt Rosemary figured out that I made the same mistake on *my* dress."

"No way," Ashley said.

"I guess I've been pretty stressed out about designing these dresses and sewing them." Emily stepped closer to the window. Grandma was parking her car in front of the shop.

"It's a lot of responsibility," Ashley said. "I understand."

They said their good-byes and then Emily opened the front door.

"Where's Rosemary?" Grandma asked.

Emily held up the extra key. "She went home. I'm locking up for her. I'll give her the key tomorrow."

Chapter Twenty-Three

Charlotte dumped her shovel load of chicken manure into the wheelbarrow, making the squawking hens jump and flutter. Emily hadn't complained once about going into town to sew on a Saturday morning. She knew the alternative was cleaning out the coop.

"Emily needs to talk to you!" Christopher stood at the back door, waving the phone.

"Ask if I can call her back in a couple of minutes." Charlotte needed to dump the load on the garden space and then she could go in and wash up.

Charlotte scooped the last of the manure off the floor.

"Grandma!" It was Christopher again. "Emily says she needs to talk with you now. Aunt Rosemary is sick again."

Charlotte leaned the shovel against the wire of the chicken coop and headed through the gate, closing it firmly behind her. She jogged across the driveway and met Christopher halfway across the lawn.

"Grandma, Aunt Rosemary is acting funny again. But this time she isn't talking at all, and her face looks funny."

"How so?"

"Like half of it is asleep. It's all saggy."

"Call 911. Tell them you're at Fabrics and Fun in Bedford. Call now. I'm on my way too."

Charlotte hung up the phone and grabbed her purse and keys, flying through the back door. "Pete!" she yelled.

Christopher was standing in the middle of the driveway with his arms out and palms up. The wind had picked up, and it had just started to rain.

"Christopher, go get Pete and Grandpa. Tell them I need one of them to come with me right now."

Christopher spun around and ran toward the shop. In another minute, Pete came running.

"It's Rosemary. Emily is calling 911."

"Dad's down by the creek, checking the water level," Pete yelled.

"Christopher, get Sam. He's in the family room. Tell him what's going on and to go down and get Grandpa. Tell him to meet us at the medical center."

Pete held out his hands for the keys, and Charlotte tossed them to him. As he backed the car out, Charlotte told Pete what Emily had told her on the phone.

"Sounds like a stroke," Pete said.

"That's what I'm thinking too."

"Poor Em." Pete turned onto the highway. "Poor Aunt Rosemary."

"AT FABRICS AND FUN, in Bedford," Emily said into her cell phone. Aunt Rosemary was slumped in her chair. "It's on Lincoln Street." Emily wished they would just send the ambulance now. At this rate, it would be faster for her to just walk Aunt Rosemary up to the medical center—if only she *could* walk.

The dispatcher asked if Aunt Rosemary was breathing.

"Yes." Her chest was moving up and down. "But she's kind of staring off into space." And she wasn't responding to anything Emily was saying.

"I'm sending the Bedford Volunteer Fire Department right now."

Emily pressed END on her phone. "Aunt Rosemary," she said, "are you okay?"

Aunt Rosemary shook her head, just slightly, and tried to say something, but nothing came out.

Tears stung Emily's eyes. Maybe she should run next door and get some help. But there might not be anyone there. She could go over to Jenny's Creamery. But maybe she shouldn't leave Aunt Rosemary.

She pulled a chair close to her aunt. Should she keep talking to her? "Thanks for helping me with the dresses. I really appreciate it."

Aunt Rosemary nodded. She could shake her head and nod. That was good. She could understand words at least, even if she couldn't speak.

Emily hoped Grandma would arrive before the EMTs. No, that was silly. She hoped someone got here fast, someone who could help Aunt Rosemary. "Dear God," Emily said silently before she even realized she was praying, "please don't let Aunt Rosemary die."

Emily wiped a tear from her eye. She didn't care if she didn't get the dresses done in time for the wedding. That didn't matter at all. She just didn't want another person she loved to leave her.

"Hello!"

She sprang to her feet. "Back here!" She scurried to the doorway. A volunteer firefighter—Emily recognized him from church but didn't know his name—hurried through the store with what looked like a big fishing tackle box in his hand. "The rest of the crew will be here soon. I was the closest," he said.

Emily pointed to Aunt Rosemary. "She started acting funny about ten minutes ago. I called my grandmother, and she said to call 911."

"You did the right thing."

"Mrs. Woodsmall," the first responder said, "can you hear me?"

As the man spoke, the front door buzzed again; Emily stepped into the shop as two other volunteer firefighters arrived, pushing a gurney through the door. Emily walked behind them back to where Aunt Rosemary sat. After that, everything seemed to move in slow motion; it felt like ages passed before Grandma and Uncle Pete arrived. He brushed past Emily, but Grandma swooped her up into her arms. Emily collapsed against her, sobbing.

Right after that, Uncle Pete and the other volunteers maneuvered Aunt Rosemary onto the gurney. Emily stepped closer, with Grandma by her side. There was definitely something wrong with Aunt Rosemary's face.

"We're going to transport her now," one of the volunteers said. "We're taking her to the Bedford Medical Center, and we'll see what Dr. Carr has to say. But it looks like this was caught soon enough that he can administer a clot deactivator. It could make all the difference for Mrs. Woodsmall."

The first responder turned toward Emily. "She has you to thank. I hate to imagine what would have happened if she'd been home alone or here on a slow day."

Emily wrinkled up her face, fighting the tears again.

"Let's go." It was Uncle Pete, directing the other volunteers to get moving with the gurney.

"We'll follow them to the medical center," Grandma said, taking Emily's hand.

"What about the store?"

Grandma stopped. "Did you give Rosemary back the spare key from yesterday?"

Emily dug in her jeans pocket and pulled it out. She'd forgotten all about the key—and so had Aunt Rosemary.

Out the door they went, locking it behind them. Then Grandma turned around. A puzzled look spread across her face. "Pete drove my car," she said. "And parked right across the street." There was an empty space where it had been. She started patting the pockets of her coat. "He must have taken it to the medical center."

Emily hadn't grabbed her coat. She pulled the sleeves of her shirt over her hands.

"Let's go see if Melody will give us a ride." Grandma hurried down the sidewalk. Emily didn't want to mention her coat; she just wanted to get to the Bedford Medical Center to see how Aunt Rosemary was doing.

DR. CARR SAT DOWN beside Grandma and Grandpa in the waiting room and cleared his throat. "Rosemary is doing as well as can be expected. I administered a plasminogen activator that can make all the difference with stroke victims. It appears that this was a ministroke and that she won't have any lasting damage."

"Can she stay here?" Grandma asked. "Or will she be transferred to Harding?"

"I'm keeping her here for tonight, but we'll revisit that tomorrow depending on how she's doing."

Grandpa's pale blue eyes glistened. "Thank you, Doctor."

"I'm just doing my job." He turned toward Emily. "I've been told it's this young lady we all should be thanking."

Emily ducked her head as Grandpa patted her on the back.

"When can we see her?" Grandma asked, standing.

"You can go in now. But just for a few minutes." The doctor shook Grandpa's hand and then Grandma's and headed down the hall.

Grandma and Grandpa started down the hall, but Emily hesitated. Grandma must have sensed her apprehension because she turned and said, "Are you all right, sweetie?"

Emily nodded. "Is she going to look, you know, funny?"

"I don't think so. She'll have an IV, and she's probably hooked up to monitors. Her face might still be a little slack. But the doctor said she's talking."

"Was this why she was sick before? Last week too?"

Grandma shook her head. "No. The doctor said that was a virus, a touch of the flu. The stroke was a separate incident."

Emily shivered. She hadn't gotten warm since the quick walk to Mel's Place and the ride to the medical center. A minute later they were in Aunt Rosemary's hospital room, and Grandma was hovering over the bed, cooing at Aunt

Rosemary, and Grandpa was standing at the end of the bed, his hat in his hands.

"Emily." Aunt Rosemary reached out her hand. "Thank you."

Emily stepped forward.

"Were you frightened?" Aunt Rosemary asked. Her wavy gray hair was pushed away from her ashen face, which still looked odd but not like it had earlier.

Emily nodded.

"I'm sorry." Aunt Rosemary squeezed her hand.

"We can't stay," Grandma said. "You need your rest."

"Can you put a sign on the door of the shop?" Aunt Rosemary let go of Emily's hand. "Say I'll be back Monday."

Grandma nodded. "I'll put a sign up—but we'll see about when you'll be back."

"Oh, I'll be back ASAP," Aunt Rosemary said. "We have dresses to finish. A rehearsal dinner. And a wedding. I can't stay down."

AS CHARLOTTE PULLED OUT of the Bedford Medical Center parking lot, her hands began to shake. Who would have thought that Rosemary would have a stroke?

After she turned onto Main Street, she felt the pocket of her jacket—yes, she still had the key—and decided to stop by Fabrics and Fun. She might as well get Emily's sewing machine and the dresses now instead of dragging everyone over after church tomorrow.

Emily was chilled and had gone home with Pete and Bob while Charlotte stayed to make sure Rosemary was settled for the night. Charlotte couldn't bear to think of what might have happened to Rosemary if Emily hadn't been with her.

Charlotte parked in front of Fabrics and Fun and slowly climbed from the car, weary to the bone. She unlocked the door to the shop and fumbled for the light switch. First she found paper and a pen under the counter by the register and made a sign that the shop would be closed due to illness. Then she headed into the back room.

Amber's dress had slid to the floor by Emily's sewing machine, and the chair was tipped over on the floor. And there was Emily's coat, draped on the back of another chair. No wonder she'd gotten chilled.

Charlotte packed up the sewing machine and gently folded Amber's dress.

As she walked to the front door of the shop, she said a prayer of thanks for her granddaughter and for her sister-in-law. Her eyes filled with tears. Both meant so much to her. "Thank you, Lord," she whispered, "that Emily was here with Rosemary."

THE NEXT DAY AFTER CHURCH, Bonnie Simons cornered Charlotte in the fellowship hall as she was rounding everyone up so they could stop by the medical center on the way home.

"I'm so sorry about Rosemary," Bonnie said, clutching her clipboard. "What awful timing."

Charlotte winced, knowing Bonnie didn't mean to sound so heartless.

Bonnie placed one hand on her chest. "How is she?"

"Stable. She had a stroke."

"That's what I heard." Bonnie lowered her voice. "But she's going to make it, right?"

Charlotte nodded, suddenly feeling choked up.

"Well, anyway." Bonnie's voice rose to normal volume. "We still have a wedding to pull off. And it's less than a week away now." She glanced down at her clipboard. "So I wanted to touch base with you about the rehearsal dinner. What can I do to help?"

"Nothing. Really. It's all under control." Charlotte turned to Christopher. "Go round everyone up and get them out to the car. I'll be right there."

"How about some details then?" Bonnie stepped forward, blocking Charlotte's escape. "Pete told me about the menu, but what about the decorations? And the dessert?"

Charlotte couldn't bear to say that Rosemary had planned to surprise Pete with her famous German chocolate cake. "Oh, dear," Charlotte said, tears springing to her eyes. "I'm afraid I can't talk right now." She swiped at her eyes as she slipped by Bonnie and followed her family out the door, the emotions of yesterday enveloping her again.

Rosemary had been like a sister to her all these years—her only sister. Next to Bob, Rosemary was the one person in her life who had been there for her every step of the way during the last forty-six years. Charlotte exhaled as she walked in the bright sunshine to the car. It was nearly warm out today. She hadn't noticed earlier because she'd been so worried about Rosemary when they'd left for church. She settled into the front seat as Bob slammed the driver's door.

"Do we have to go in and see her?" Christopher asked from the backseat, wedged between Sam and Emily.

"It depends on how she's doing," Charlotte answered.

"If she's not feeling up to it, none of us will see her. But Grandpa and I want to talk with the nurse, at least."

As it turned out, none of them saw Rosemary because she was sleeping. The nurse said she'd had breakfast and was communicating just fine. But she needed her rest.

"Why don't you call later this afternoon?" the nurse said.

The boys seemed relieved when Charlotte and Bob came out to the car and told them they would have to wait to see their aunt, but Emily was obviously disappointed.

"When can she go home?" she asked.

"That's a good question," Charlotte said.

Bob backed out of the parking space. "She'll need to come out to the farm," he said, shifting into drive. "She won't be able to be by herself for a while."

"Maybe Emily could stay with her nights," Charlotte said, thinking out loud.

"No, she needs to come out to the farm." Bob's voice was firm.

AFTER THE SUNDAY DINNER DISHES had been loaded into the dishwasher, Emily announced that she was going to go ride Britney.

Charlotte started to speak but caught herself.

"I'll sew later," Emily said as she pulled on her boots. "I have it all figured out. I've started on Amber's dress, so

I should be done by Tuesday. I've got it down now. Then I'll only have to hem the dresses."

Picking up the kitchen scraps, Charlotte said, "Sounds good. I trust you on this." She walked outside with Emily, happy to be in the fresh air.

"Hey, Grandma." Sam stood at the barn door. "Would you come take a look at Snowflake? He doesn't look so good."

"I'll be there in just a minute." She unlatched the chicken coop and stepped inside. Whew. The smell of manure nearly overwhelmed her. She'd forgotten to ask the boys to empty the wheelbarrow.

Charlotte shooed the chickens away from her feet and began distributing the scraps, taking little short breaths as she did to avoid the smell.

Her mind wandered to the week ahead. She planned to paint the dining room tomorrow. The walls were all scrubbed and ready, and she had purchased the paint. She had planned to get started with the painting Saturday afternoon, but Rosemary's trip to the medical center had delayed that project. Still, she was sure it wouldn't take long. She would have to wait until after the carpet cleaners came in the morning. But then she'd also have to see how Rosemary was doing. Charlotte might need to be at the hospital with her sister-in-law—or maybe she'd be bringing her home to Heather Creek Farm.

When she entered the barn, all three of the children were hovering around the calf, who lay on the ground at the far end of his pen, nearly buried in the straw.

"Step back," Charlotte said. The calf was probably tired.

Or lonely. She bent down. "Eeew," she said. "He smells worse than the chicken coop. Sam, when was the last time you changed his straw?"

"This morning. Honestly. And last night too. He's been really stinking up the place even though I've been giving him plenty of water."

Charlotte took a step backward. "He probably has scours."

"Has what?"

"A bacterial infection that calves get."

"Why don't you just call it that?"

Charlotte shook her head. "It's just what it's called; that's all. Where's Pete?"

"Out in the field. He's going to vaccinate the calves tomorrow, and he's taking a head count," Sam answered.

"One of you go get him," Charlotte said. "Tell him Snowflake needs a round of antibiotics."

"I'll ride Britney out to tell him." Emily clambered over the gate of the pen.

"Thanks," Charlotte said.

"Is he going to be okay?" Sam asked as Emily left.

Snowflake had been ill for at least a day and he was small; he definitely had two strikes against him. "I don't know," Charlotte answered. Pete could hoist him into his truck and take him into the vet tomorrow if he wanted, but financially Charlotte didn't think it would be worth it. Sam's emotional state was another concern.

BACK IN THE HOUSE, Charlotte called the medical center and was put through to Rosemary's room.

"I don't know why they didn't just wake me up when

you stopped by," she said. "I only fell asleep because I was bored."

They chatted for a few minutes and then Rosemary said, "So can you come and get me?"

"When?" Charlotte asked.

"Right now." Rosemary giggled.

"Now?"

"Yep. Dr. Carr just left. He said I'm doing fine. But I need to come back tomorrow afternoon to get my blood pressure checked, just to see how it's doing."

"So you can go home? This afternoon?"

"Well," Rosemary said, "that's the catch. He said I shouldn't be alone for a couple of days—you know, just in case."

"We expected that you would come out here."

"Are you sure? You have the rehearsal dinner. The dresses. The wedding. The kids."

Charlotte walked toward the family room, carrying the cordless phone. "Of course I'm sure. I'm on my way." But she wasn't quite on her way. First she woke up Bob.

"Come help me change the sheets on our bed, quick," she said.

Bob yawned. "Char, what's going on?"

"Rosemary is going to come stay here for a few days, and I need your help. She needs to stay in our room. We'll sleep in Pete's. He can bunk with Sam."

He yawned again.

"Bob, I can't do all this by myself. For this next week, you'll need to help me. A lot."

Chapter Twenty-Four

"I'm sorry to make you stay back here," Charlotte said to Rosemary the next morning, placing a breakfast tray on the bed. Rosemary was getting around well enough with her cane to come to the table, but Charlotte didn't want her to have to dodge the carpet cleaners.

Rosemary chuckled. "I've never had breakfast in bed before—except at the medical center, of course." She jabbed her spoon into the bowl of oatmeal. "And I see you're feeding me Bob's diet, not the kids'."

"You see right," Charlotte said. "We want you around for a long time to come." She stepped back. Rosemary's left eye drooped just a little, and she was a little unsteady when she walked, but those were the only signs that she'd had a stroke. "The cleaners are doing the carpet in the hall first. So then you'll have access to the bathroom."

"What about your room?" Rosemary asked, looking around. "Or don't your carpets get dirty?"

Charlotte smiled and then said, "Not like the rest of the house." She'd planned to get all the carpets cleaned on the first floor but decided not to juggle Rosemary around. It wasn't worth it. What the house really needed, and Emily had pointed it out—again—this morning, was new carpet. But that was low on her priority list. Actually it hadn't even made the list.

"Tell Bob to come chat with me when he's done with his breakfast," Rosemary said, stirring her coffee. It was decaf—doctor's orders.

"Oh, he's out already—helping Pete vaccinate the calves." Rosemary shook her head. "He's too old for that."

"Well, he's just shooing them into the chute. Pete's the one doing all the work." Charlotte stepped toward the door. "Do you need anything else?"

"No." Rosemary picked up her napkin. "Except to say thank you." Her eyes glistened. "I don't know what I would do without you."

"DAD!" PETE YELLED. "Watch that calf." One of the bigger calves snuck around, wiggling through just before his dad swung the gate shut.

Dad lunged after it, but not in time. The calf bucked as it took off down the field.

"Never mind. I'll get it later," Pete said. They had forty calves to vaccinate who were six weeks or older. He'd have another forty or so in another six weeks, including Snowflake—if the little guy made it. Sam had begged Pete to call the vet last night and then again this morning when Pete gave the calf his second dose of antibiotics. But the runt wasn't worth calling the vet over or hauling in; he'd either make it or he wouldn't. They'd already spent enough on calf formula.

Pete tipped his head to the clouds. It was going to rain; he was sure of it.

"We should have done this Saturday." Dad stood at the back of the corral. "When Sam and Christopher could have helped."

"We were a little busy Saturday afternoon, remember?"

"That's right," Dad said, rechecking the gate.

But he was right. It would have been much easier with one more person.

"You could go get Mom."

"Nah. The carpet cleaners are coming any minute. And she has Rosemary to look after."

"Okay." Pete clapped his leather work gloves together. "Let's get started." He'd been vaccinating calves for as long as he could remember. He had rounded them up this morning on the four-wheeler with Toby's help. He had even gotten them into the corral alone—but he couldn't do this next part without some help.

His dad stepped behind four calves and waved his arms. One veered helter-skelter to the left, but the other three headed toward the chute.

"Yeehaw!" Dad yelled, waving his arms again. A second calf peeled off and ran to the opposite side of the holding pen, but Dad got two of the calves into the crowding pen and then clapped his hands until they filed into the chute where they calmed down.

Pete secured the first calf in the head gate and then grabbed the prepped syringe from the table. He reached through the slats of the chute to stick it into the calf's shoulder. The calf jerked as Pete pushed the needle in, but he had it out before the calf could jerk a second time. Pete pulled his hand back through the slats and dropped the syringe into a bucket. One down. Thirty-nine to go.

After the fifteenth calf, Dad said he needed a break. "Come get a cup of coffee," he said to Pete.

Pete shook his head. "Why don't you send Mom out? Maybe she could give you a break."

Dad kept walking away. He used to work all day, sixteen hours at a time, riding Pete for not working hard enough. Now look at him—off for a cup of coffee at 10:30 AM. Pete stepped out of the chute. Oh, well. He needed to prep more syringes anyway.

He made his way through the holding pen, climbed the fence, and then entered the barn through the tack room, opening the old refrigerator and taking out a tray of vaccine. Next would come branding, worming, weaning, and later, breeding and dehorning. It was a never-ending process. He opened the cupboard and took out another box of syringes. If he'd been smart about things, he would have gone to school to become a vet. Maybe. But being a farmer was the next best thing. Plus he didn't have to put up the money to pay for all that college and then to buy a vet business or start his own.

He peeked in on Snowflake. The calf appeared to be asleep. Pete waited for a few seconds. Yep. His side was rising and falling; the little guy was still alive.

He started back to the holding pen. He could try to get a couple through on his own. He placed everything on the table and loaded a few syringes. That's where Mom was a big help because she usually got them all ready and handed them to him through the slats of the chute. Then he went back into the holding pen. The calves were bawling now, and their mamas were gathering around the fence, starting to get worked up.

Mom had always been a big help on the farm. Dana, with her teaching, wouldn't be available like that. But the teaching was a good thing; it meant medical insurance for both of them and a retirement plan for Dana. Those were both things his parents could use now. But it had been nice all these years to have Mom around, working beside them when they needed her. He sighed. That was another good thing about teaching. Dana would be around during the summers, at least.

She seemed to be doing better now as far as the wedding planning, but every once in a while she would get a faraway look in her eyes, and he would get nervous that maybe she didn't really want to marry him.

He shooed two calves into the crowding pen, and forced them into the chute, walking behind them until he could reach the syringes. The bigger calf kicked up his heels, and Pete came down on his back end firmly. "No need to get rough," he said, and then reached forward and stuck the needle in the calf's shoulder.

The calf bucked backward at an angle, pushing Pete against the side of the chute. Then the other calf joined the ruckus, kicking his heels into Pete's ribs, sending the unused syringe flying out of his hand into the holding pen.

"Oh, good grief," Pete moaned. "Did you really have to do that?" He pushed against the calves, reading the ear tag on the one that didn't get the shot. "Well, number 204, I'm going to let you go for now, but just you wait. I'll be back." He groaned as he opened the chute and let the calves through.

He'd broken ribs twice before, both times during branding. Never from giving calves their vaccinations. He started to laugh and then stopped. Maybe his ribs were just bruised; either way they hurt like crazy. He wasn't going to tell Dana. She might understand, but Mrs. Simons would think he had done it on purpose. Or she would lecture him for vaccinating calves the week before the wedding or something like that. Pete bent down to pick up the syringe he'd dropped.

"Hey." Dad stood at the edge of the holding pen. "You're moving like an old man."

"Yeah, well, a calf just took me out."

"Were you daydreaming about a new tractor?"

"As a matter of fact, no." Pete headed back to the chute. He hadn't given the tractor a thought in a couple of weeks. That had just been a distraction—and a cost that was about the same as building a house for him and Dana. So what if their tractor was as old as he was? As long as Dad was around to tinker with it, it would keep running.

"Were you thinking about your wedding?"

Pete shook his head. "Actually, I was thinking about my marriage."

"Well, that's more important than a tractor or a wedding." Dad had what almost appeared to be a look of approval on his face as he took his place back in the holding pen. "Your mom will be out in a minute. The cleaners are almost done, and Rosemary is napping."

"Oh, good," Pete said, slipping back into the chute. "Maybe we'll be able to finish today after all." He groaned again as the next couple of calves came through, and when he reached for the syringe he yelped.

"Hold on, son," Dad said. "Your mom will be here in a minute. Maybe you should go into town and have Dr. Carr look at those ribs."

Pete shook his head. Dad really was getting soft. He knew better than anyone that nothing could be done by a doctor for broken ribs that they couldn't do at home. He'd have Mom tape them when they stopped for lunch.

"WHAT ARE YOU GOING TO DO for centerpieces for the tables?" Rosemary asked as Charlotte taped Pete's ribs, the first-aid kit open on the table.

"Centerpieces?" Charlotte hadn't given them a thought. "Flowers, I guess. Maybe tulips?" Hers hadn't bloomed yet. "I could ask down at the flower shop and see if they could order some." Dana was having white tulips for the ceremony. Maybe Charlotte could order a variety of colors for the tables.

"What's your theme?" Rosemary asked.

"Well, spring." She hadn't thought beyond that.

"You could have Bob make something." Rosemary shifted her weight on the dining room chair and leaned forward on her cane. "I know. How about little birdhouses? I saw the cutest pattern in a magazine at the store."

Charlotte tore another piece of tape and began sticking it onto Pete. He winced but didn't say anything. "Bob wouldn't have much time to make them." Honestly, Charlotte didn't want to start another project.

"Christopher could help. I could too—with the painting."

"Actually, I still wanted to get the walls in here painted." Charlotte looked around at the dingy off-white dining room.

"It's too late," Rosemary said. "It would still smell like paint by Friday. Believe me, I've made that mistake before."

Charlotte hadn't thought about that.

"Just wash the walls," Rosemary said.

Charlotte wanted to cry. "I have." She'd scrubbed them until she was afraid if she scrubbed any more she would strip the paint.

"Oh." Rosemary squinted and then scrunched her face up into a smile. "Maybe the stroke messed up my vision."

The back door slammed open and Bob walked into the kitchen. "What's for lunch?" he asked, rubbing his hands together.

"Sandwiches." Charlotte had been out helping with the calves half the morning. It wasn't like she'd had time to whip up a hot meal. "Uh, Bob," she said as he walked toward the hall. "Would you take off your boots? The carpet just got cleaned."

"Oh, right." He backtracked to the mud porch.

Charlotte tugged the last piece of tape into place. "There you go, Pete. Hopefully everything that can go wrong has now." She smiled. "At this rate you should have a perfect wedding day."

He smiled, just a little, pulled down his T-shirt and gingerly put on his work shirt. "You know, I think the birdhouses are a great idea if Dad will do it."

"Do what?" Bob asked.

"Make—what? five?—birdhouses," Rosemary answered. "I'll bring you the pattern this afternoon."

"You need these when?" Bob stood in the middle of the kitchen in his stocking feet.

"Friday," Charlotte answered, her voice calm.

"It'll be easy, Bob," Rosemary said. "I'm sure you have all the wood you need. You might need to pick up some paint at the hardware store."

"You could take Rosemary to her appointment this afternoon to get her blood pressure checked and then stop by," Charlotte said, "after you see the pattern."

He started walking again. "I'm getting a nap this afternoon. You can stop by the hardware store if you want. I'll get started later on the birdhouses if I decide to do them." He was halfway down the hall, his voice trailing off.

"Well, at least if he's making birdhouses he won't be working on every vehicle we have," Charlotte said. "Or looking for others." Maybe he wouldn't be turning the place into a junkyard after all.

"I'LL BE RIGHT BACK," the nurse said to Rosemary, leaving the blood pressure cuff on her arm and heading out the door.

"Must not be good," Rosemary said, slumping back in the chair.

"Do you feel all right?" Charlotte asked.

"Fine and dandy," Rosemary answered. "You know, a little tired. But that's all."

Dr. Carr returned with the nurse. "Your blood pressure is high," he said. "Let's take it a second time just to be sure."

The nurse pumped the bulb, and the cuff swelled. She put her stethoscope on Rosemary's arm and listened silently, watching the gauge. "It's still 190/110."

"I'm afraid we're going to have to readmit you until that blood pressure comes down," Dr. Carr said. "It was okay yesterday."

"Oh, goodness," Rosemary said. "This is getting ridiculous."

"I'll go back to the house and get your things," Charlotte said.

"Don't forget to give Bob the pattern and the paint." Luckily they'd gone by Fabrics and Fun and the hardware store before the appointment.

Charlotte nodded in agreement, the lump in her throat keeping her from speaking.

Later, as she headed out of the farmhouse with Rosemary's bag in her hand, the phone rang.

"Grandma." It was Emily. "Can you do me a favor? I need some more fabric paint to finish a school project. Do you still have the key to Aunt Rosemary's shop? The one I gave you the other day."

Charlotte exhaled. "Emily, Rosemary is back in the hospital."

"But she was doing fine."

"Her blood pressure is high again. I'm on my way back into town with her things."

"Can you pick me up at school? Can I go see her?"

"Sure. I'll be there right away." She hung up the phone

and then turned toward the family room. "Bob," she called out. He let out a snore. "Bob," she said again.

His head jerked up, his reading glasses falling from his face into his open hand.

"I'm taking Rosemary's things to her. The pattern and paint are on the table."

He nodded.

"Could you get started on the birdhouses—or else on dinner?"

He sat up straight.

"There's hamburger thawing on the counter. You could start the meatloaf." She might as well suggest it.

He stood. "I'll get started on the birdhouses."

"Five of them."

He stretched.

She took a step toward the kitchen.

"Char." Bob was standing now. "Just keep letting me know what I need to do. You know, I don't see things, but as long as you tell me, I'll help." He smiled. "Just don't make me fix dinner." He reached out his hand for hers, and Charlotte gave him a quick hug, leaning against his solid barrel chest.

Bob took a deep breath. "I'll go in this evening and sit with Rosemary a spell."

Fifteen minutes later, as Charlotte waited for Emily in the school parking lot, Sam approached the car, and she rolled down her window.

"Is everything all right?" he asked.

"Rosemary is back in the hospital."

"Oh." Sam frowned. "That's too bad. How is Snowflake?"

"Okay." But the truth was, she wasn't sure. She hadn't checked on him all day. Surely Pete had. She was trying to remember if Pete had given the calf his bottle after lunch.

Sam smiled again. "When I saw your car I thought you'd come to tell me he'd died."

Charlotte shook her head.

"Well, Arielle is coming out again to see him. Is that all right?"

Charlotte paused. "As long as you give Christopher a ride home. And is there anything I need to know about you and Arielle?"

Sam shook his head. "No, Grandma, it's not like Arielle and I are going out or anything. She still thinks I'm a jerk—you know, about colleges and stuff. She likes Snowflake; that's all."

Charlotte waved at Emily coming down the stairs. "Well, check in with Grandpa when you get home. And take Arielle home right away and then see what you can do to help Grandpa with the birdhouses."

"With the what?"

"Just ask him, okay?"

Emily hopped in the car, and Charlotte told Sam goodbye and shifted into reverse.

"Did Aunt Rosemary have another stroke?" Emily asked, pulling her seat belt across her chest.

"No," Charlotte answered. "It's just her blood pressure."

"Do you think she'll let me get more fabric paint? It's to finish up a school art project."

"Probably," Charlotte answered. "You can talk with her first." She still had the key; she just wanted Rosemary to know what was going on.

A few minutes later, Charlotte placed Rosemary's bag on the chair by her hospital bed, and Emily asked about the fabric paint.

"Of course you can get more fabric paint," Rosemary said. "Honestly, I don't know why I'm in here. I feel fine."

"Will you be out by Saturday? In time for the wedding?" Emily's eyes pooled with tears.

"Of course, honey." Rosemary hooted and then said, "I'd have to be dead to miss that wedding."

SAM SWUNG OPEN the barn door for Arielle and stepped aside, but Christopher scurried in first.

"Will you help me with the ladder?" Christopher asked, running toward the stack of hay bales.

"In a minute," Sam called after him, latching the door behind him.

Britney whinnied in the distance. Sam squinted in the dim light as a swallow flew down from the rafters. It looked as if several of the horses had come in from the pasture. It was cold again; that was for sure.

"I'd be surfing by now if we still lived in San Diego," Sam said. Arielle gave him a pathetic look, and he immediately regretted what he had said. It was such a showy thing to say. No one in Nebraska cared anymore that he used to live in California.

He opened the gate to the pen. Snowflake was in the corner again, lying on his side. The place didn't smell too bad. So maybe the antibiotics were working.

"Is he okay?" Arielle asked.

Sam nodded, hoping he wasn't lying; he kneeled down in the straw. "Hey, Snowflake," he said, rubbing the calf's side. He jerked his hand back and quickly stood up. "Christopher! Go find Uncle Pete."

It must have been the tone in Sam's voice that yanked Christopher off the hay bales. A second later Sam heard the tack room door slam.

"What's wrong?" Arielle stood with her hands to her face.

"I don't know," Sam said. But he did know—the calf was dead. Tears sprang into his eyes.

"Oh, Sam," Arielle said. "I'm sorry." She understood what he couldn't say.

He stuffed his hands into the pockets of his jeans and swallowed hard. He wasn't going to cry in front of Arielle.

Neither one of them said anything. Arielle bent down and touched Snowflake's black head. Sam couldn't bear the thought. He took a step backward.

He heard Uncle Pete's boots on the concrete at the back of the barn. "Sam!"

"He's in the calf pen, like I told you." Christopher's high-pitched voice carried through the barn.

"What's going on?" Uncle Pete asked as he opened the gate to the pen.

"The calf is dead," Arielle answered.

Uncle Pete paused and then wrapped his arm around Sam's shoulder. "Sorry, bud."

Sam's head dipped against his uncle's chest, and he felt Uncle Pete stiffen, but then he drew Sam close, holding his head, and Sam began to cry. He expected Uncle Pete to say

"I told you so" or "This is part of living on a farm," but he didn't. He just patted Sam's back.

"It wasn't like he was doing great earlier," Uncle Pete said as Sam carried the calf's corpse through the barn. "But he was alive when I gave him his bottle after lunch."

Arielle and Christopher trailed behind, a funeral procession in the making.

"We'll put his body over by the tractor," Uncle Pete said, stopping behind the barn. "I'll dig a hole with the backhoe later."

Sam started to hand Snowflake to Uncle Pete, but he stepped away. "I can't carry him; some other calves beat me up today." He patted his ribs.

Sam lowered the calf against the barn. "Will coyotes or anything get him?"

"Nah."

"What about vultures?"

Uncle Pete shook his head. "I really am going to bury him today. That I can do with broken ribs. I'll get Grandpa to help."

"Bye, Snowflake." Christopher bent down and patted the calf's head, but then a robin flew by and he stood again. "I'm going back into the barn to check on that nest." Christopher spun around as he spoke, but Sam caught him by the arm before he could take off.

"Hold your horses," he said. "You are not going to climb that stack of hay bales and look out that window. Do you hear me?"

Christopher tried to pull away, but Sam held on tighter.

"Did you just hear Uncle Pete say he got hurt today? And Aunt Rosemary is back in the hospital. And Snowflake is dead. It's called Murphy's Law. Stay away from that nest—unless you're looking at it from the ground outside the barn." Sam pointed to the windowsill and then grabbed Christopher's chin with his hand and thrust it upward. "Look. They're not sitting up there, so that means no eggs. Got it?"

"Let go of me," Christopher whined.

"Not until you promise not to climb that stack to the top and do that gymnastic thing you do."

Christopher didn't answer.

Sam squeezed harder.

"Okay," Christopher wailed.

Sam let go. He was afraid to look into Arielle's eyes, afraid she might think he was a bully.

Uncle Pete was smirking, but he didn't say anything, and even if he had been going to speak up he was cut short by Grandma's car turning into the driveway. Christopher ran toward it, waving his bare hands, his unzipped jacket flying out on either side of him.

"Are you ready to go home?" Sam asked Arielle.

"Yes," she said softly and walked beside him to his car.

Neither one of them said a word on the way to town. As Sam reached the city limits, the sky began to spit rain, just enough to smear the windshield. When he pulled into Arielle's driveway she cleared her throat gently and then said, "I'm sorry."

"Thanks," he answered.

She opened the door. "I'll see you at school." Then she turned and hurried toward her house as the rain began to pour.

Chapter Twenty-Five

I'd have to be dead to miss that wedding. Emily shivered as she stood at her bedroom window. Grandma said that Aunt Rosemary's stroke had just happened. That a blood clot had lodged in one of the veins in her brain. But Emily couldn't help but wonder if the clot had built up because she was stressed, because she and Aunt Anna were asking her for help with the sewing and then Mrs. Simons was in and out of the shop twenty times a day looking for just the right lace and then Grandma needed help with the rehearsal dinner.

Aunt Rosemary had been under so much pressure, but it had been the sewing that seemed to really stress her out.

Honestly, Emily didn't care that much that the calf had died. She felt bad for Sam, but the calf was going to die sooner or later anyway. It wasn't like when Stormy was born and they were afraid she might die. Horses lived a really long time. But Snowflake was going to end up as meat, and Uncle Pete and Grandma had reminded Sam of that nearly every day. It was Sam's own fault that he had got so attached to it and then dragged Arielle out to see it and all that.

So a dead calf was one thing. But Aunt Rosemary's ordeal was entirely different.

If she got out of the hospital again, Emily would volunteer to stay with her at night. She could call 911 again. She wouldn't hesitate a second time. And if she had it to do all over again, she wouldn't have volunteered to make the dresses. Sam was right; she'd done it for attention. Sure, she liked to design and sew, but she had volunteered to make the bridesmaids' dresses so that everyone would ooh and aah and tell her what a good job she had done. In her pre-design fantasy, she had never imagined that she would stress out herself and Aunt Rosemary and Miss Simons and Grandma and Dana's mom in the process.

Sam's car turned into the driveway, and she could see the rain streaming in front of his headlights. She stepped back to her desk and slumped down in front of the sewing machine. She was dreaming in royal blue now, seeing the color every time she closed her eyes. Ashley had painted her Georgia O'Keeffe flower a royal blue today in art, and Emily nearly got nauseated looking at it.

She pulled the fabric paint out of her book bag and then the T-shirts for Miss Simons and Uncle Pete for their rehearsal. She'd decided to add blue tulips to the design.

There was a knock at the door and then it flung open. "Time to eat," Christopher bellowed. "We're having hot dogs—well, one of those veggie things for you." He was gone before she could wiggle from her chair. Grandma must be feeling as stressed out as she looked, Emily thought, heading down the stairs.

GRANDPA SAID A SHORT PRAYER and then speared a hot dog. "I haven't had one of these since—" He looked straight at Grandma. "I can't remember the last time I had a hot dog."

Grandma just smiled and passed the store-bought potato salad to Sam.

Grandpa didn't say another word. In fact everyone concentrated on dinner until Uncle Pete came into the house. He went straight for the bottle of pain reliever in the kitchen and took what looked like a handful.

"Come eat," Grandma said.

"Can't," he groaned, standing off to the side of the table. "I shouldn't have buried the calf, even though it was with the backhoe."

Everyone looked at Sam, but his face was turned down toward his plate as he shoved half his hot dog into his mouth.

"In fact, I'm going to go lie down," Pete said. "I'll see if sleep's a possibility or if I should just get used to the idea of being in pain."

"If you can't sleep, I have some birdhouses—"

"Bob," Grandma said.

Christopher grabbed a second hot dog. "I helped Grandpa today," he said. "I wish that robin family would move into one."

"Birdhouses aren't for birds," Emily explained, cutting her veggie dog into bites. "They're for decorations."

"Birds can nest in them," Grandma said with that protective edge to her voice.

"When have you ever seen an actual bird live in a birdhouse?" Emily asked. No one answered. "My point exactly," she muttered.

"Does anyone want to go in with me to visit Rosemary?" Grandpa asked, pushing back his chair.

"I need to work on the dresses," Emily said.

"I have homework." Sam grabbed another hot dog from the plate.

"I thought I'd get started on painting the birdhouse you made today," Christopher said.

Grandpa looked a little disappointed.

"I need to stay home and get caught up on things," Grandma said. "Because I need to go into Filly's Flower Shop tomorrow to order some tulips to display around the birdhouses."

"How much will that cost?" Grandpa asked.

"Hush," Grandma said. "We've waited a long time for Pete to get married. We can splurge on some tulips."

AFTER SHE FINISHED the dishes, Emily trudged back up the stairs and finished the tulip designs, leaving the T-shirts to dry on her floor. Then she pinned the interfacing around the neckline of Amber's dress, but when she sat down at the sewing machine she felt so tired she decided to rest for a few minutes first. The light hurt her eyes so she flicked off the overhead, leaving her desk lamp on. A little nap was what she needed, just enough to let her stay up for the rest of the evening. If she sewed until eleven she was sure she could finish Amber's dress...

"Emily." Grandma stood beside the bed, her hand on Emily's shoulder.

Emily's eyes flew open. She had slept so soundly it took

her a minute to get her bearings. "Is it time for school?" Emily asked, alarmed that she'd overslept.

"No, sweetie. It's nine o'clock." Grandma's hand brushed across Emily's forehead and then rested there. "Honey, you're burning up."

Grandma said she'd be right back with the thermometer and asked Emily to get into her pajamas. She did, trying to swallow several times as she pulled on the pajama bottoms. Her throat felt thick and raw. She crawled back under the covers and then Grandma knocked again, slipped through the door, and inserted the thermometer into Emily's mouth.

"I'll be right back," Grandma said.

Emily snuggled under the blankets as she gripped the thermometer with her lips. She didn't feel like she was burning up—she felt like she was freezing.

Grandma returned just as the thermometer began to beep. "One hundred two," she said. "I'll bring you some Advil and water." She stroked Emily's head. "I think Pete has it too."

"Oh, no," Emily said.

"We have a few days until the wedding," Grandma said. "Hopefully Dana won't come down with it."

"Or Aunt Rosemary," Emily added.

Grandma nodded and then sat down on the edge of Emily's bed. "Mind if I pray?" Grandma asked.

Emily felt a smidge of relief. "Please do," she answered.

Grandma prayed that Emily would be well soon and would have enough time to finish the dresses. She prayed for Pete and for Rosemary. She prayed that God would comfort Sam. And then she said, "And most of all, help us to love and cherish each other during this special time in the life of our family—uh, families. Amen."

Emily echoed with her own "amen" as Grandma stood.

"I'll be right back." Grandma pushed the button on the thermometer and slipped off the plastic sleeve as she headed to the door.

Later that night, as Emily fell in and out of sleep, she kept seeing bolts and bolts of royal blue fabric in her mixed-up dreams, flowing over the fields, the top of the barn, the house. In one dream she was riding Britney, but the horse became entangled in the fabric and started to fall. Emily woke up with a start. Her throat was worse. She could hardly swallow.

EARLY TUESDAY MORNING Charlotte sat in her chair, her Bible in her hands, reading 1 Corinthians 13:4: "Love is patient, love is kind. It does not envy, it does not boast, it is not proud."

Charlotte bowed her head. *Proud.* Feeling apprehensive about hosting the rehearsal dinner was due to her pride and her caring about what Bonnie Simons thought. She smiled a little in her humility. "I'm sorry, Lord," she whispered.

With Rosemary in the hospital and Pete and Emily sick, her dingy walls didn't seem nearly as important. Loving each other was what was really important—being patient and kind. Not being proud. She recalled a verse from Proverbs that included the line, "love covers all offenses." She closed her eyes. "Lord," she whispered, "please cover my pride with your love."

At nine o'clock sharp, Charlotte had Emily and Pete at the clinic, and, as she expected, they both had strep throat. Maybe someone at church had been contagious—or at the medical center on Saturday. Maybe both Emily and Pete had been more stressed out than Charlotte had realized. She counted the days on her fingers. *Tuesday. Wednesday. Thursday. Friday.* Thanks to the antibiotics, they should both be okay in time for the rehearsal, at least. But she wasn't sure if the dresses would be ready by then.

As Dr. Carr handed her the prescription he pushed up the sleeves of his lab coat. "I have some good news to counteract the bad." He smiled. "Rosemary's blood pressure has stabilized. She can go home."

"Home to her house? Or to ours?"

"Can someone stay with her? I don't want her exposed to strep."

"Of course. I'll ask around," Charlotte said. "I'll be back for her, okay? After I get these two settled." She wasn't worried about coming down with strep. It seemed as if people either got it or they didn't, and in all her years she never had. But she remembered that Pete had had a few previous bouts back in high school.

She got Pete and Emily into the car and headed toward the pharmacy.

"Thanks, Mom," Pete said.

She smiled at him. It was one of the last motherly things she would do for him in her own home, Lord willing. Her smile grew into a grin.

"What?" Pete said, a sheepish look on his face.

"I'm just so happy you are getting married," Charlotte

said. "Married to Dana after all these years. Who would have thought?"

"And you're not stressed out? You know, by me and Em being sick and Rosemary—"

She interrupted him, not being able to bear hearing the whole list. "Everything will work out." She wasn't going to dare add, *because everything that could possibly go wrong already has gone wrong.* That old saying sounded good—but wasn't true. Still, she knew that even if more things did go wrong, she could trust God to work them out.

Back at home, Hannah called as Charlotte was thinking about what to fix for lunch. When she told her friend they needed someone to stay with Rosemary, Hannah immediately volunteered.

"I insist," Hannah said. "Frank will be fine by himself for the rest of the week. Of course I'll do it."

Charlotte said, "Dr. Carr said just for a couple of nights, as long as her blood pressure stays down and she doesn't seem confused or anything."

"It's a deal," Hannah said. "You have way too much on your plate right now. It's my pleasure to help. You get her settled, and I'll take care of a few things around here and then I'll head into town."

As soon as Charlotte hung up, the phone rang again. This time it was Dana. "How is Pete feeling?" She must have talked with him the night before.

Charlotte filled Dana in on the doctor's visit as she walked into the family room.

"Strep!" Dana's voice rose as she spoke. "Now what?"

"He'll be fine by the wedding," Charlotte said. "Here's

Pete. I'll talk to you soon." She handed Pete the phone and headed back into the kitchen to start a pot of soup.

A few minutes later Pete slumped into the kitchen with the phone. "Dana wants to talk with you again."

Charlotte dried her hands and took the phone.

"Well, Mom will be relieved that you think everything will come together." Her voice didn't sound as serious as it had earlier. "If not, I think she'll be the next one admitted to the medical center."

"Honestly, Dana, these things work out. It's God's way of making us stronger."

Dana chuckled a little. "I hate to think what he's toughening me up for." Then she laughed and said good-bye.

Charlotte hurried into the family room. Pete was on one end of the couch, and Emily was on the other. "It's soup for both of you and then bed," Charlotte said.

A FEW HOURS LATER, as she headed back out to the car to go get Rosemary, Bob came ambling out of his shop, a birdhouse in his hand. "What do you think?" he held it up.

It looked even better than the picture in the magazine. It was a white birdhouse with a church steeple. Outside of the small round opening Bob had stuck two little blue birds.

"Where'd you get those?" Charlotte asked, pointing at the birds.

"Rosemary gave me the key to her shop last night. These were in the craft section." He beamed.

"These will make wonderful centerpieces," Charlotte said.

"And it's a good thing you're making them because I forgot to order the tulips. But I'm not even going to bother now." She would see about getting some moss from Rosemary.

"I thought I'd make a little picket fence too," Bob said. "If I have time. And maybe write 'Dana and Pete, March 28' on the side."

"Lovely. Bob, you could start a business making these—" But then she let her voice trail off. She wasn't really serious. "As a hobby, I mean." Charlotte gave him a quick peck on the cheek.

Charlotte climbed into her car, thinking about Dana laughing before she hung up the phone. Maybe she would make it as a farmer's wife after all; she certainly was rolling with the punches when it came to her wedding. And speaking of daughters-in-law, she had a favor to ask of her first one. Hopefully Anna would be game to help. And it was high time she contacted Melody too, and put her on crisis alert.

She knew Hannah would do more than stay with Rosemary. Charlotte needed her friends and family now more than ever. Maybe that was why she was feeling so calm. She had finally felt overwhelmed enough to ask for help—and to not care what Bonnie Simons thought of her, her home, or her family.

"OF COURSE I CAN HELP with the food," Hannah said, dropping her overnight bag on Rosemary's camelback sofa. "How about my twice-baked potatoes? Pete loves those."

"Perfect," Charlotte answered. Rosemary was settled in her bedroom for a nap, and Hannah had just arrived.

"And I can make Rosemary's German chocolate cake. I have the recipe."

"Thank you," Charlotte said, giving her friend a hug.

"What else can I do?" Hannah asked.

"How are your sewing skills?" Charlotte reached for the doorknob.

"Charlotte Stevenson, you know sewing makes me crazy. I can't even remember the last time I took that infuriating machine out of its case."

Charlotte smiled. "I was joking. Actually, there's one more thing you could do."

"Anything."

"How are your baby-holding skills?" She let go of the knob.

"It's been a while," Hannah said. "But if it's for a worthy cause..."

"It is." Charlotte opened the door. "I'll fill you in on the details tomorrow. I need to make a phone call first."

Chapter Twenty-Six

On Thursday during lunch Sam wedged between Jake and Paul in the cafeteria, settling his tray on the tabletop. It was taco day. Grandma had hardly cooked all week, and he was famished.

Across the room, Miss Simons was speaking with Ms. Carey, the art teacher.

"There's your new auntie," Paul teased, pushing his stocking cap off his forehead.

Sam ignored him. He felt sorry for Emily, having to go to the same school where a relative was a teacher for the next two years. At least Sam would be off to college. Maybe.

"Hey." It was Arielle, behind him.

He tried to spin around but instead managed to slam into Paul and then Jake. He untangled himself and finally just stood and turned to face her.

"How are you doing?" she asked.

"Fine." Sam would never understand girls. He had three classes with her. Why didn't she just ask after class instead of waiting until he was with his friends?

"I really am sorry about Snowflake." Her blue eyes were all watery.

Jake snickered, sounding like a horse.

"I know you were really sad," she continued.

Paul slapped the table and turned around too. "Who are you guys talking about?"

"Sam's calf. He bottle-fed it, but it died a couple of days ago."

Jake hooted.

Arielle wrinkled her nose. "Knock it off, you guys. Hey, I'm going to sit over there." She pointed across the room, over by where Miss Simons was still standing. "Care to join me?"

"Uh." Sam reached for his tray. "Sure."

"Snowflake," Paul said, his hand patting his chest. "Sam, why didn't you tell us?"

Sam ignored them. For once he didn't care what his friends were saying. "See you later," he said, trailing after Arielle.

As they sat down, Miss Simons waved at Sam and hurried over. "How was Pete this morning?"

"Fine," Sam said, trying to remember if he'd seen Uncle Pete before he left for school. Oh, yeah. He had come into the kitchen and asked what was for breakfast just as Sam was leaving. "He seems a lot better."

"Well, I plan to come out to the farm this afternoon, as long as he's not contagious."

Sam nodded. Grandma had said last night that both Uncle Pete and Emily weren't contagious anymore, because they'd been on their medication long enough. She'd finally let them out of their rooms and stopped boiling their dishes. But Grandma still seemed a little paranoid. Miss Simons gave Sam a little wave and headed to the food line with Ms. Carey.

"What's going on?" Arielle asked.

"Strep."

"Oh, no."

He nodded. "Things have been crazy. Mostly this wedding. I'll be really glad when it's over."

Arielle opened her carton of milk, smelled it, and then dropped her straw in.

"Uncle Pete's been too busy, with getting ready for the wedding and everything. He hasn't been able to keep up with things around the farm."

"Like the calf?" Arielle asked.

Sam nodded.

"Sometimes things just happen though," Arielle said.

Sam felt a catch in his throat and looked away for a second before he cleared his throat and said, "Well, there's always too much going on with the whole Stevenson clan, if you know what I mean. It's a model of chaos." They'd been studying dysfunctional families in sociology.

Arielle laughed. "Actually, I think your family is one of the best families I know. Sure, there's always a lot going on, but everyone is always pitching in and helping out." She leaned forward a little. "Count your blessings, Sam." Then she covered her mouth. "I'm sorry. I didn't mean—"

He knew she was feeling bad that she'd said that to someone whose mother had died, someone who didn't have much of a relationship with his father. "No," he said. Then he paused. "You're right." And she was. Sam picked up his taco.

Then he put it back on his plate. "Hey." He looked at Arielle, who was squirting a packet of hot sauce onto her own taco.

Old feelings were welling up in him, and he decided to go out on a limb. "I was wondering if you have any plans this Saturday. I think I'm allowed to bring a guest to Uncle Pete's wedding, and I thought, you know, since you've been out at the farm a lot lately, you might want to go."

Arielle took a deep breath. "To the wedding?" she asked.

"Yeah, I mean, if you want. I'll be on duty as a groomsman," he said. "But I'd love to have you there if you're willing to come."

"I'd like that very much," she said, her beautiful blue eyes shining.

Sam picked up his taco again and took a bite. He wasn't sure what this meant, but he knew he liked having Arielle around, and it would be fun to have her as his date on Saturday, regardless of where things went from there.

EMILY WOKE UP to a darkening bedroom and voices downstairs. For a second she was afraid she'd slept through the night and it was time for the rehearsal. The dresses! She still needed to sew the pleated trim on hers and Michelle's and sew the fringes on the shawls.

She grabbed her cell phone and looked at the date. Whew. It was still the twenty-sixth. *Thursday evening.* She could still sew on the trim tonight and then hem Amber's dress tomorrow—after Amber arrived and had her fitting.

She stood and swallowed. Her throat was fine, and she didn't ache anymore. For the first time in two days, she wasn't even tired. She grabbed her jeans and sweatshirt. A shower sounded good. As she headed to the bathroom, she caught a glimpse of Jennifer at the bottom of the stairs. That explained the voices she'd heard. Aunt Anna had come over to get Grandma to help her with the kids so she could sew.

A half hour later, her hair wet, Emily ventured down the stairs. First she bumped into Hannah in the family room walking back and forth with Will. Then Jennifer and Madison ran past her, chasing Lightning. "Where's Christopher?" Emily asked.

Madison giggled. "Painting birdhouses with Sam and Grandpa."

Emily continued into the dining room. Grandma, Aunt Anna, Aunt Rosemary, and Ms. Carey all sat at sewing machines around the table, and Miss Simons was pinning fringe onto a shawl.

"Hi, Em," Grandma said. "How are you feeling?"

"Lots better. What's going on?"

"We're finishing the dresses," Miss Simons said.

Emily pulled out a chair next to Ms. Carey, her face growing warm, this time from blushing, not from fever.

"You were in good shape to finish," Miss Simons said, "if you hadn't gotten sick."

"And I know you planned to sew tonight," Grandma added, "but none of us wanted you to overdo it."

"Thanks," Emily said. Ms. Carey was sewing the trim on Emily's dress.

Aunt Anna glanced at Emily but kept sewing. She was finishing the neckline on Amber's dress, and she seemed to be doing a good job. "These little cap sleeves are sweet," she said to Miss Simons.

"They were Amber's idea; she didn't want bare arms. They've been a pain though—right, Em?"

Emily nodded.

Will began to fuss, a little at first and then louder. Hannah made her way into the dining room.

"He's hungry," Aunt Anna said, reaching for him.

"Are Madison's and Jennifer's dresses done?" Emily asked.

Aunt Anna nodded. "I finished them last weekend while Bill bonded with his baby boy."

Emily turned toward Aunt Rosemary, feeling a little like Dorothy after her return to Kansas. "How are you?"

"Fine. My blood pressure is good again. Hannah gets to stay at her own house tonight."

"Can you go to the wedding?" Emily asked, remembering her aunt's comment about having to be dead not to attend.

"Of course," Aunt Rosemary said, her eyes dancing.

"Charlotte, would you pass me the pins?" Miss Simons asked.

It was the first time Emily had heard Miss Simons call Grandma by her first name, and it sounded funny. But if Miss Simons could call Grandma "Charlotte," then Emily could probably start working on calling Miss Simons "Aunt Dana." But not at school. Never at school.

Emily reached for a shawl and a portion of fringe in the middle of the table and sat down in the chair by Grandma.

Grandma tossed a pincushion to Miss Simons and then scooted one toward Emily. As she started working, the conversation steered to the rehearsal dinner. Grandma had done all the grocery shopping earlier in the day. Sam and Uncle Pete were going to move the furniture tonight, as long as Uncle Pete felt up to it, and Sam and Grandpa were going to pick up the tables and chairs from the church tomorrow.

"Is Uncle Pete sleeping?" Emily asked.

"No." Grandma glanced at Miss Simons. "He's been working all afternoon."

Miss Simons shrugged. "He gets to make his own decisions for one more day."

All the women laughed.

THEY HAD PIZZA for dinner—pre-baked ones from the grocery store. When Grandma lined them up on the kitchen counter, Grandpa didn't look pleased, but he kept silent.

Christopher kept Madison and Jennifer entertained talking about the robins' nest. "I thought the mama bird had laid eggs," he said, and then, ducking his head so Grandma couldn't hear, he added, "but I checked and it hadn't. And now I haven't seen the birds for a few days."

"Grandma said it was too early for the mama robin to lay eggs. She said robins lay their eggs in April," Emily said.

Christopher shrugged. "Maybe they went off to build a new nest. That one is on a slant. Maybe they're afraid their babies will fall out."

Jennifer nodded.

As Emily chewed her pizza, Ms. Carey approached. "The dresses are really beautiful," she said. "And the design is pretty difficult. How did it go?"

Emily swallowed. "Honestly?"

Ms. Carey nodded.

"I messed up a lot—starting with cutting the sleeves out, then with sewing them on, then with the neckline and all those funky pleats. It's been quite an experience."

"Quite a learning experience?" Ms. Carey smiled.

Emily nodded and took another bite of pizza, thinking of Ashley. She'd suggested that Emily ask for help much sooner. What if Emily had told Miss Simons the dresses were too much way back then? Maybe she would have asked Ms. Carey to help her from the beginning. It would have saved all of them a lot of grief. Ashley had been right.

And she'd been right that Emily shouldn't have been deceptive in what she told Miss Simons about her progress —or lack of it. Then Emily had lied to Grandma, Miss Simons, and Michelle about forgetting the dresses the night of the shower, all because she was so intimidated by Bonnie Simons.

Emily walked into the kitchen and slipped her paper plate into the garbage. She needed to apologize to Grandma and Miss Simons tonight—and tomorrow to Michelle for making her drive back to Bedford. And to Bonnie Simons for lying to her too. She headed back into the dining room, silently praying that God would give her an opportunity to apologize.

AFTER DINNER, Aunt Anna closed up her sewing machine and rounded up her kids, taking Will from Hannah.

"Thanks." Aunt Anna looked appreciative.

"Hurry on home," Grandma said. "We don't want to be worried sick about you again."

Aunt Anna smiled. "I was fine that night—just stopped to get a cup of tea on the way home."

"Well, you scared Bill out of his wits," Grandma said.

"I'm not tired tonight," Aunt Anna said. "And besides, I have my chatterboxes to keep me awake." She patted her girls on the head, one by one. "And my crying machine," she said, giving Will a squeeze.

Emily gave her aunt a quick hug and thanked her. "Is your cell phone on?"

Aunt Anna dug in her purse and pulled it out. "Yes. And it's even charged." She laughed.

After Aunt Anna left, Miss Simons said, "I need to go too. Mom's insisting on one last planning meeting. But first, how about if I help Sam with the furniture so Pete doesn't have to?"

"Oh, please," Uncle Pete said, overhearing her from the family room.

"Oh, please what?" She turned toward him, standing with her hands on her hips. "Your ribs hurt so badly you can hardly kiss me."

"Don't kiss him!" Grandma said, her eyes wide. "We don't want you to get sick too!"

Miss Simons waved her hand in front of her face. "You said he's not contagious."

"Well, just in case." Grandma stood up from the table. "Let's all move what we can right now. Those who feel like they can."

"I can help," Emily said, slipping on her shoes.

She held one side of an end table, sharing the load with Christopher, as they carried it across the lawn. The weather had changed since she'd gotten ill. Tonight was warmer, almost balmy. In the glow of the porch light she could see Grandma's yellow tulips blooming along the side of the house.

"We're putting it in the shed," Christopher said. "Grandpa said there are fewer mice in there."

Emily shuddered.

Uncle Pete stood at the shed door, directing traffic. "Thanks, you two," he said.

Emily smiled at her uncle.

A minute later, as they headed back to the house, she turned back toward Uncle Pete. Miss Simons stood next to him, saying something. Then she stood on her tiptoes and kissed his cheek.

Emily cleared her throat. "Aunt Dana."

Miss Simons turned around, a look of surprise on her face.

"I need to apologize to you." Emily turned toward Grandma. "And to you too, Grandma. Could I speak to both of you in private?"

They followed her toward the side of the shop, and Emily took a deep breath, said a silent prayer, and then asked their forgiveness. Both were gracious, but—funny thing—neither seemed surprised.

"THE HORS D'OEUVRES are all on the table," Hannah said, walking into the kitchen with an empty tray. Melody had delivered crab cakes, portobello turnovers, and artichoke dip in the late afternoon, along with her broccoli salad.

Charlotte stood in the dining room and surveyed the scene. A buffet table stood where the couch usually was, the tables were all covered with royal blue tablecloths and featured the white birdhouses, and white lights, intertwined with greenery, were draped around the walls. The overhead lights were low—a trick Melody said to use—so no one would ever guess that every wall in the house needed to be painted.

As the wedding party helped themselves to the appetizers, Charlotte and Hannah delivered the rest of the food to the buffet table—except for the rib eye steaks, which Pete and Bob brought in ceremoniously.

After the blessing, everyone dished up and then sat down at the tables. Amber sat by Emily, and Charlotte overheard her say again how much she liked her dress and how impressed she was that it had turned out so well. Sam and Brad, Pete's groomsmen, sat at another table with Bill and Anna and their girls.

Dana and Pete, wearing their bride and groom T-shirts, sat at the table closest to the kitchen with Bonnie and Chuck, Grandma Maxie, and Bob and Charlotte. Chuck commented on the steak, asking if, since they were all going to be family, the Simonses would have access to the Stevensons's beef.

"Of course," Bob boomed. "A quarter beef? Half a beef? How much can you eat in a year? Just give Pete your order."

Charlotte wondered if he would really be that generous, but just the thought made her happy—and made Chuck Simons ecstatic.

"Have you made an offer on that tractor yet?" Chuck asked Pete, his steak knife in midair.

Pete reached for Dana's hand that was resting on the tabletop. "I have better things to spend my money on. Dad's going to have to keep that old antique running for a few more decades."

Bob leaned back in his chair. "That I can do." He chuckled. "Long after I turn over the farm to you, I imagine I'll still be tinkering with that old thing."

"Mom, did I tell you that Pete's parents got married at Bedford Community Church too?" Dana asked.

"Yes, I believe you did." Bonnie cut her steak.

"What were your colors?" Dana asked.

"Yellow," Charlotte answered.

Bonnie craned her neck, looking into the kitchen. Was she looking at the butter-cream cupboards and the old yellow Formica? "So, you've liked yellow all these years?"

Charlotte smiled. "We were married in the fall. You know, back then there weren't as many choices when it came to flowers. We had yellow glads, and that's why I chose the color."

Charlotte reached over for Bob's hand. "Rosemary was my maid of honor. Of course we just had a cake-and-punch reception—nothing fancy like what you've planned at the Goldenrod Bed and Breakfast."

Bonnie's eyes lit up, and she put down her steak knife. "You know, everything is going to be just perfect. The ceremony. The reception. It's a dream come true." She stopped and then hurried on. "For Dana. And for Pete."

Pete looked as if he wasn't hearing a word his soon-to-be-mother-in-law was saying.

"Well," Grandma Maxie said, tucking a stray hair back with a pin, "perfect isn't everything." She caught her granddaughter's eye, and Dana smiled.

"Bonnie," Charlotte said, shifting in her chair. "Tell us about your wedding. I've been remiss not to ask about it."

"Well." Bonnie shot a look at Chuck. "It was very small and, uh, intimate."

Chuck laughed. "And in Vegas. At one of those chapels on the Strip, one of about two way back when."

"You're kidding." Dana nearly choked. "You never told me that."

"And it was a very, very nice wedding, I might add," Grandma Maxie said. "I saw the photos."

Chuck put his arm around Bonnie. "I wouldn't have had it any other way, because I got what I wanted. Thirty five—"

"—six," Bonnie interrupted.

"Years of marriage," Chuck said. "Don't you agree, Bob and Pete—"

Pete was staring at the man who would soon be his father-in-law.

"—that the details of the wedding don't matter? It's the marriage that counts." He squeezed Bonnie tightly.

"Oh, you," she said. "Knock it off." But she smiled just a little through teary eyes.

Then Dana whispered to Pete, loudly enough that Charlotte could hear, "That's what I've learned through all of this too."

Pete raised his water glass in a toast. "To marriage."

Grandma Maxie, all smiles, was the first to bump Pete's glass. "To marriage," she boomed.

Pete brushed his face against Dana's hair. "Have I told you lately how happy you make me?"

Dana looked him straight in the eyes and said, "Tell me again."

"You make me the happiest man in the world," Pete said.

"Well." Grandma Maxie put her water glass down. "I dare say, we have a happy marriage in the making."

Chapter Twenty-Seven

"You look beautiful," Charlotte said, kissing Dana's cheek. And she did. Her dark hair was piled atop her head, the lacy veil her mom had made was perched on top, and Melody's designer dress fit her like a glove. She looked like a 1940s movie star.

"Time for photos!" Bonnie Simons chirped. "We're going to start with the Stevensons."

"Oh, dear," Charlotte said. "Rosemary isn't here yet. She wasn't quite ready when I stopped by, so Sam went to her house to wait for her."

Bonnie crossed her arms.

"Mom, it's okay," Dana said. "Let's do our family first."

A cloudy expression passed over Bonnie's face, but then it softened. "That will work."

"Yoo-hoo!" Rosemary was coming down the hall toward her, speeding along without her cane.

Charlotte rushed to meet her. "How are you?"

Rosemary dabbed at her eyes just a little. "You know, Dr. Carr warned me that I would feel more emotional than usual."

Charlotte linked arms with her sister-in-law, and they headed toward the church sanctuary.

"Anyhoo," Rosemary said, "I keep thinking about your wedding day. When we were all so young." She sighed. "And you know what? It wasn't that long ago. These kids have no idea..." Rosemary's words trailed off, and then she broke into a smile. Charlotte smiled with her.

CHARLOTTE TOOK A FEW deep breaths as she waited beside Bonnie Simons at the back of the church. Pete had just finished seating Grandma Maxie and then had slipped into the pastor's study.

Bonnie still seemed stressed. She stood with her eyes glued to Christopher as he lit the candles, which were surrounded by greenery and white tulips. Charlotte smiled. *One. Two. Three. Four. Five.* There, he was done with the first set. He shook a little as he walked across the platform to the second candelabra.

"He's nervous," Bonnie commented.

"The flowers are lovely," Charlotte answered. And they were. The greenery wound around the metal of the candelabra and up each candle.

"Oh, dear," Bonnie said, craning her neck. "I think he's started a fire."

Sure enough, smoke was coming from the first candelabra.

"Bob," Charlotte said, but he was standing toward the hallway and didn't hear her. She turned back to the front, and there was Pete, scrambling up the side aisle, taking the steps in one stiff leap and pulling the smoking greenery away from the display. He dropped it on the floor, jerking his fingers back, stomping the fire out, and then blowing all of the candles out.

Christopher stood frozen in horror in front of the second, unlit candelabra.

Pete turned toward the guests. "Candlelight ceremonies are overrated, don't you think?"

Everyone laughed.

"Christopher, buddy, we're good. Come on."

Christopher whispered, "Sorry," as he headed to the steps.

"Could we have a glass of water up here?" Pete asked, glancing down at the floor. "Just to be sure."

Charlotte turned toward Bonnie, expecting her to be horrified, but she was laughing. She reached for Charlotte's arm. "That was my fault," she said. "I'm the one who wound the greenery too close. Poor Christopher."

On the platform, Bill, Brad, and Pete were all bent down, and Pete was sprinkling water from a glass he held in his hand.

As Christopher came through the doors to the foyer, Bonnie caught his arm. "I'm sorry," she said.

He wasn't shaking anymore. He was smiling. "That was wild," he said.

Christopher handed Bonnie the antique candlelighter. She put it against the wall of the foyer, right next to her clipboard.

Sam asked Charlotte if she and Bob were ready to be seated.

"Wait until the cleanup crew is finished," Bonnie said, her voice still lighthearted. She bent closer to Charlotte and said, "You know, what I regret about my own wedding isn't that it was small or even that it was in Vegas—although for years I thought that was it. What I regret is that I didn't have family who could be there with me. People I could count on. All these years I thought it felt flat because it was so simple, but that wasn't it at all. And the family I did have—Chuck's parents—I ignored. But they never held it against me."

Charlotte took Bonnie's hand and squeezed it. "Well," she said, "you have plenty of family now." With that she motioned to Bob and took Sam's arm. They started down the aisle, Christopher tagging along behind them, and slipped into the pew in front of Anna, Will, and Rosemary. A moment later, Sam seated Bonnie. Next, Madison and Jennifer came down the aisle, sprinkling white petals, their dresses perfectly pressed and the long blue ribbons in their perfectly French-braided hair flowing behind them. The bridesmaids and groomsmen followed.

Then came Dana and Chuck, the father towering over the daughter, a smile spread across his face. Dana leaned in toward him, Daddy's little girl for one last moment. Charlotte turned toward the front. Pete stood at the top of the aisle, looking as if he were about to cry.

As Pastor Nathan began the vows, Charlotte tried to keep her eyes on the wedding party. The bridesmaids' royal blue dresses looked gorgeous from her vantage point, perfectly complemented by the groomsmen's bow ties and cummerbunds. Pete had never looked so handsome in his life.

Pete held Dana's hands and repeated after Pastor Nathan. "I, Pete Stevenson, take thee, Dana Simons, to be my wedded wife ... to have and to hold from this day forward, for better or for worse ... for richer or for poorer, in sickness and in health, to love and to cherish ..."

Charlotte took Bob's hand, thankful for all the work he had done to help get them to this point. He'd shown his love, helping her during the past week just as he had done throughout the years.

Forty-six years ago she hadn't understood what the words *love* and *cherish* truly meant. Now she knew it was so much more than just loving and cherishing Bob. Everyone she loved who still lived on this good earth was in the church right now. She wanted to stand up and look at each one. To say, "I love and cherish you, each of you."

And now Pete and Dana were beginning their own journey. She could only pray that their lives would be filled with as much family, community, commitment—and chaos—as her own.

About the Author

Leslie Gould is the #1 bestselling and Christy-Award winning author of over forty novels. She and her husband, Peter, live in Portland, Oregon and enjoy hiking, traveling, and hanging out with their adult children and young grandson.

A Note from the Editors

We hope you enjoyed this volume in the Home to Heather Creek series, published by Guideposts. For over seventy-five years, Guideposts, a nonprofit organization, has been driven by a vision of a world filled with hope. We aspire to be the voice of a trusted friend, a friend who makes you feel more hopeful and connected.

By making a purchase from Guideposts, you join our community in touching millions of lives, inspiring them to believe that all things are possible through faith, hope, and prayer. Your continued support allows us to provide uplifting resources to those in need.

Whether through our online communities, websites, apps, or publications, we strive to inspire our audiences, bring them together, and comfort, uplift, entertain, and guide them.

To learn more, please go to guideposts.org.

Find inspiration, find faith, find Guideposts.

Shop our best sellers and favorites at
guideposts.org/shop

Or scan the QR code to go directly to our Shop